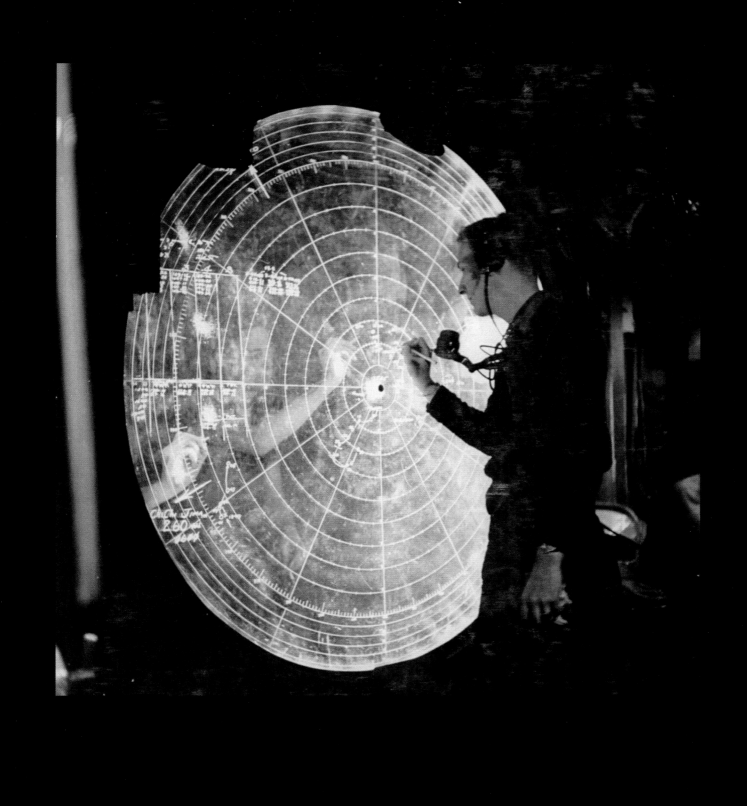

AIRCRAFT CARRIERS

THE ILLUSTRATED HISTORY OF THE WORLD'S MOST IMPORTANT WARSHIPS

MICHAEL E. HASKEW

ZENITH
PRESS

CONTENTS

PROLOGUE

At 7:55 a.m. on December 7, 1941, the quiet of a Sunday morning was shattered as aircraft of the Imperial Japanese Navy devastated the US Pacific Fleet moored in Pearl Harbor and other military installations on the Hawaiian island of Oahu. The attacking planes were launched from the decks of six aircraft carriers that had furtively sailed to within 230 miles of Hawaii to initiate the surprise air assault.

When it was over, no doubt remained: The aircraft carrier was ascendant in naval warfare, eclipsing the dreadnought battleship as the primary offensive weapon on the world's oceans. World War II in the Pacific, prosecuted across thousands of miles of open sea, was won and lost with the deployment of carrier air power.

Pearl Harbor was the brainchild of Adm. Isoroku Yamamoto, commander-in-chief of Japan's Combined Fleet. A naval veteran, Yamamoto had experienced combat, losing two fingers on his left hand during the epic Battle of Tsushima, when the Imperial Navy defeated the Russian Baltic Fleet in 1905 during the Russo-Japanese War. He studied at Harvard University and served as a naval attaché in Washington, D.C. A staunch advocate of carrier air power, he earned his pilot's wings at the age of forty.

Yamamoto was aware that carrier-based aircraft of the British Royal Navy in the Mediterranean Sea had inflicted serious damage on the Regia Marina, fascist dictator Benito Mussolini's fleet, on November 11, 1940, while the big Italian battleships rode at anchor in the presumed safety of Taranto Harbor.

Yamamoto knew that American industrial capacity could eventually doom Japan to defeat. A prolonged war was out of the question. He conceived the attack on Pearl Harbor as the best option to gain a swift victory, cripple the US Navy in the Pacific, and win a negotiated peace with the Americans. He warned, "Give me six months, and I will run wild in the Pacific. After that, I make no guarantees."

Without the aircraft carrier, Yamamoto's bold strike at Pearl Harbor, tactically expanded and led by two brilliant staff officers, Lt. Cmdrs. Minoru Genda and Mitsuo Fuchida, could

never have taken place. The powerful Japanese task force that delivered the sledgehammer blow left Hitokappu Bay in the Kurile Islands on November 26, 1941, under the command of Admiral Chūichi Nagumo.

On that fateful Sunday morning, six Japanese carriers—*Akagi*, *Kaga*, *Sōryū*, *Hiryū*, *Shōkaku*, and *Zuikaku*—hurled 353 dive-bombers, level bombers, torpedo bombers, and fighter planes against the Americans in two waves. Despite several warnings that might have alerted US forces, the Japanese achieved complete surprise. Within minutes, the attackers had strafed and bombed American installations at Hickam Field, Bellows Field, Schofield Barracks, Kaneohe Naval Air Station, and Ewa Marine Corps Air Station.

At Pearl Harbor, the Japanese planes ravaged Battleship Row adjacent to Ford Island. When the last bomber turned back toward the carriers, four American battleships were sunk and four more heavily damaged. Hit by five torpedoes, the *Oklahoma* capsized, trapping hundreds of sailors below decks. The *West Virginia* was struck by seven torpedoes and two bombs and settled upright into the muck of the harbor's shallow bottom. Two torpedoes and a bomb tore through the *California*. The *Arizona* was demolished by a modified fourteen-inch naval shell fashioned for delivery as an aerial bomb, which penetrated the battleship's forward magazine and ignited a tremendous explosion, killing 1,177 sailors and marines.

The battleships *Tennessee*, *Maryland*, *Nevada*, and *Pennsylvania* were heavily damaged, as were the cruisers *Honolulu*, *Raleigh*, and *Helena*; the destroyers *Cassin*, *Downes*, and *Shaw*; the seaplane tender *Curtiss*; and the repair ship *Vestal*. The elderly minelayer *Oglala* and target ship *Utah* were also sunk. In addition, 165 American aircraft were destroyed and another 128 damaged, most of them on the ground. A total of 2,403 Americans died. Japanese losses were minimal: 29 aircraft, a fleet submarine, five midget submarines, and 185 killed.

Although the blow was staggering and the US armed forces required months to regain full strength, the Japanese triumph was far from total. Fearful of an American counterstrike,

Aircraft fly in diamond formation over the newest *Nimitz*-class aircraft carrier, the USS *Ronald Reagan*, at the conclusion of the ship's commissioning ceremony. The attack on Pearl Harbor underscored the carrier's preeminence. In the decades since, the aircraft carrier has served as a primary means of projecting military might around the world. *US Navy photo/Photographer's Mate 2nd Class Charles A. Edwards Jr.*

Admiral Nagumo declined to mount a third air attack against Pearl Harbor and ordered his ships to retire. The Japanese raiders had failed also to demolish the oil storage tanks at Pearl and had left machine shops and other repair facilities relatively untouched, allowing the Pacific Fleet to operate on a limited basis early in the war and to recover more rapidly.

For the Japanese, the most critical misstep simply involved bad timing. The Pacific Fleet's aircraft carriers were not present at Pearl Harbor during the attack, surviving unscathed. Fuchida remembered that on December 6 a message was received at sea. It noted, "No balloons, no torpedo defense nets deployed around battleships in Pearl Harbor. All battleships are in. No indications from enemy radio activity that ocean patrol flights being made in Hawaiian area. *Lexington* left harbor yesterday. *Enterprise* also thought to be operating at sea."

Although the *Lexington* was lost during the Battle of the Coral Sea in May 1942, her planes participated in the sinking of the Japanese carrier *Shōhō* and damaged the *Shōkaku* during the fight. A month later, aircraft from the deck of the *Enterprise* took part in the Battle of Midway, in which four of the Japanese carriers that had wrecked Pearl Harbor—*Akagi*, *Kaga*, *Sōryū*, and *Hiryū*—were sent to the bottom of the Pacific.

By the time of the Pearl Harbor attack, the aircraft carrier had existed as a weapon of war for less than a quarter of a century. During World War II, the carrier became the preeminent warship afloat. Naval strength was largely defined, and still is today, by the number of operational carriers a nation had put to sea along with their complements of lethal aircraft.

For decades, the aircraft carrier has served as a nation's primary means of projecting military might around the world. In the modern era, these massive ships, largely self-sufficient, and their escorts are capable of delivering decisive strikes against enemies across the globe. The story of the aircraft carrier is the story of innovative, visionary thinking among naval leaders and the introduction of one of the few conventional weapons systems that is capable of influencing the outcome of a conflict with its very presence.

INDISPENSABLE VESSELS

In December 1907, President Theodore Roosevelt ordered the United States Navy to conduct an ambitious circumnavigation of the globe. The ensuing operation lasted until February 1909, projecting American naval might around the world like no other great power had done before. Nicknamed the "Great White Fleet," sixteen battleships flexed the military muscle of Roosevelt's modern US Navy.

At the same time that the Great White Fleet made its historic fourteen-month voyage, the eyes of some naval officers and enterprising civilians had already turned to an innovation that was destined to change the character of warfare at sea. Soon after the pioneering flight of the Wright Brothers at Kitty Hawk, North Carolina, in 1903, armed forces began considering the military potential of the airplane.

Captain Henry C. Mustin, Naval Aviator No. 11, pilots his Curtiss Model F flying boat from the flight deck of the armored cruiser USS *North Carolina* off Pensacola, Florida, on November 5, 1915. The flight was significant as the first assisted by catapult from the deck of a ship. The name of the warship is plainly visible emblazoned on its stern. *National Archives*

In this editorial cartoon from 1909 by artist William Allen Rogers, George Washington, Uncle Sam, and Theodore Roosevelt welcome the Great White Fleet home from its world cruise. President Roosevelt dispatched the US Navy squadron of modern battleships on its historic voyage in a projection of military might that sent a clear message: the United States had become a global naval power. *Library of Congress*

While the airplane's capacity for reconnaissance, observation, and directing gunfire was promising, the question remained as to how it might work with ships at sea. The seaplane and the flying boat were conceived to marry air and naval operations, but their potential was limited. Aircraft that could take off and land on the deck of a ship, however, offered tremendous possibilities. Visionary men seized the opportunity, and by midcentury the aircraft carrier would eclipse the battleship as the preeminent weapon of naval warfare.

Among the foremost advocates of naval aviation, Glenn Curtiss was born in Hammondsport, New York, on May 21, 1878. As a young man, he was an employee of Eastman Kodak and became familiar with the camera, which led to a significant photographic record of his early aircraft designs and exploits. In business for himself by the age of twenty-three, Curtiss was building bicycles in Hammondsport when his need for speed led him to develop a small gasoline engine that was then mounted on one of the bicycles.

Curtiss converted his business to manufacturing motorcycles, and his engines gained a reputation for excellence. By 1904, he was supplying them to Thomas Scott Baldwin, who used them to power his balloons and dirigibles, including the *California Arrow*, which made the first controlled circular flight in America that year. In 1907, Curtiss established a world speed record of nearly 137 miles per hour on the hard sands at Ormond Beach, Florida.

In the autumn of that year, Alexander Graham Bell, known most widely as the inventor of the telephone, invited Curtiss to travel from Hammondsport to Baddeck, Nova Scotia, Bell's summer home. Bell considered Curtiss one of the world's leading experts on high-performance engines and asked Curtiss to join his fledgling Aerial Experiment Association (AEA). Bell explained that the AEA was formed with "the purpose of constructing a practical aerodrome, driven by its own motive power, and carrying a man." Curtiss was named the group's director of experiments.

Above: A Curtiss Pusher aircraft sits tethered to a wire apparatus during preparations for flight testing. The Curtiss Pusher was one of a relative few versatile early aircraft that were adaptable for naval operations, serving as a platform for pioneer aviators in carrier takeoffs and landings as well as seaplane flights. *National Archives*

Right: Curtiss flying boats lie moored adjacent to the shore in Hammondsport, New York. Hammondsport was the hometown of Glenn Curtiss. After he returned from Baddeck, Nova Scotia, in 1909 following work with Alexander Graham Bell's Aerial Experiment Association, Curtiss began designing aircraft in Hammondsport. *National Archives*

When the AEA dissolved two years later, Curtiss began designing airplanes in Hammondsport. Two of his models, the Pusher and a Pusher Flying Boat, were placed in production, and pontoons were added to the land-based Pusher to produce the world's first operational seaplane.

Meanwhile, Curtiss gained flying fame, winning the International Gordon Bennett Race in August 1909 and permanent possession of the Scientific American Trophy after capturing it for the third time in 1910, upon completion of a 150-mile flight from Albany, New York, to a safe landing on Governor's Island in New York Harbor. He won the Collier Trophy in consecutive years for his successes with the seaplane in 1912 and the flying boat in 1913.

Glenn Curtiss was also a businessman, and he realized that the best opportunity to keep his aircraft manufacturing concern commercially viable was to demonstrate to the US military that aircraft were essential to future operations. Both the army and the navy hesitated to commit substantial

Above: Fliers churn the water near the US Navy's facility at Pensacola, Florida. Their aircraft is an early biplane designed by Glenn Curtiss. One of the foremost proponents of naval aviation in the United States during the early 1900s, Curtiss was also instrumental in the development of carrier air operations. *National Archives*

Right: Glenn Curtiss, shown at the pilot's wheel of one of his early biplanes, was instrumental in the development of the seaplane and in promoting naval aviation. Through his efforts, he earned the title of America's "Father of Naval Aviation." *Library of Congress*

resources to aviation, and by 1909 only one Wright airplane was in service with the army. The navy purchased its first aircraft, an A-1 Triad seaplane, from Curtiss in 1911. Curtiss was friendly with a number of senior naval officers, and with their help he was able to stage thrilling demonstrations that changed the course of history. In the process, he also earned the title of America's "Father of Naval Aviation."

Working with Captain Washington Irving Chambers, the US Navy officer responsible for aviation research and development, Curtiss devised a plan for an airplane to take off from the deck of a navy warship. One of his demonstration pilots, twenty-three-year-old Eugene B. Ely, volunteered to pilot the Pusher, powered by a fifty-horsepower engine. At the Norfolk Navy Yard in Virginia, workmen sawed and hammered together an improvised flight deck stretching eighty-five feet long and twenty-four feet wide with a five-degree downslope across the bow of the cruiser USS *Birmingham*. The makeshift platform was only thirty-seven feet above the waterline.

On the morning of November 14, 1910, the fragile airplane was hoisted aboard the ship, and the *Birmingham* steamed out of Norfolk into Hampton Roads near the mouth of the Chesapeake Bay. Rain pelted down from a leaden sky. The weather had improved sufficiently by 3:00 p.m., and although the cruiser was supposed to have been underway when Ely was at the controls, she rode at anchor off Old Point Comfort. The impetuous Ely seized the opportunity, climbed into the pilot's seat, revved the engine, opened the throttle, and roared down the flight deck in front of a throng of sailors at approximately 3:15.

The Curtiss Pusher leaped from the deck and took a precipitous dip, its wheels and propeller striking the water. Ely wrestled for control and then regained precious altitude as water sprayed his goggles and virtually blinded him. The potential for an airplane to take off from the deck of a ship had been proven, but Ely's craft was seriously damaged. He had hoped to fly a considerably greater distance but was in the air for fewer than five minutes before setting the plane down on the beach near Fortress Monroe just three miles away.

Pilot Eugene B. Ely sits in the cockpit of a biplane. Note the position of the engine directly to his rear, the configuration of wires and struts that held the plane together, and Ely's controls, which resemble an automobile steering wheel. On the afternoon of November 14, 1910, Ely piloted the Curtiss Pusher that succeeded in the first launch of an aircraft from the deck of a naval ship. *National Archives*

Ely was disappointed at the brevity of his flight. Nevertheless, naval carrier aviation was born.

The following day, the *New York Times* reported, "Eugene B. Ely's successful flight in a biplane yesterday from the deck of the scout cruiser Birmingham through a fog five miles to shore will have the effect, it is said here to-day, of interesting the Secretary of the Navy as a valuable and practical addition to the navy. . . . Ely is considered to have solved one-half of aeronautics at sea; he has launched himself successfully from the deck of the ship. The other problem is how to bring the airships back to the deck without alighting first in the water. It is not believed, however, that this part of the problem will be left unsolved long."

The newspaper was right. A month later, Secretary of the Navy George Meyer, who had initially opposed the development of naval aviation, petitioned for additional funding for such projects. As the navy devoted more resources to aviation, Ely took to the air a second time on January 18, 1911. Taking off from the deck of a ship was one thing. Landing presented quite a different array of challenges, including how to stop the plane if and when it actually touched down.

Above: The US Navy cruiser *Birmingham* churns a white wake while steaming southward along the Atlantic coast of the United States. The *Birmingham* played a pivotal role in early aircraft carrier aviation history when a short flight deck of eighty-five feet was constructed on its bow to accommodate the historic launch of pilot Eugene Ely's Curtiss Pusher in Chesapeake Bay on November 14, 1910. *National Archives*

Opposite: Commander Theodore Gordon Ellyson, the first US Navy officer designated as an aviator, and later identified as "Naval Aviator No. 1," sits at the controls of the first aircraft acquired by the navy, a Curtiss Pusher seaplane. This photograph was taken in February 1911. Ellyson was a member of a small group of naval officers ordered to undertake aviation instruction with the legendary Glenn Curtiss. Ellyson, who later flew with Curtiss and consulted with him on aircraft design, was killed in a plane crash in 1928. *National Archives*

Captain Chambers was again instrumental in the demonstration, set this time for San Francisco Bay. At the Mare Island Navy Yard, workmen fashioned a flight deck 133 feet 7 inches long and 31 feet 6 inches wide across the afterdeck of the armored cruiser USS *Pennsylvania*, covering the stern's eight-inch gun mount. The problem of halting the careening airplane as it landed was solved with the installation of a series of twenty-two manila hemp rope lines stretched across the temporary deck at three-foot intervals and anchored on either end by fifty-pound sandbags. In theory, a hook attached to the plane's tail would grab at least one of the lines, slowing it sufficiently to roll safely to a stop. Canvas awnings were erected at each end of the flight deck and along the sides to corral the plane in the event of a crash.

On that January morning, the changeable weather in San Francisco Bay altered the plan for a while. Captain C. F. Pond of the *Pennsylvania* had intended to get the cruiser underway

continued on page 18

Above: While a crowd of sailors and guests watches intently and many more observers look on from the shore, Eugene B. Ely touches down on the flight deck of the armored cruiser USS *Pennsylvania* in San Francisco Bay at approximately 11:00 a.m. on January 18, 1911, completing the first successful landing of an aircraft aboard a warship. As Ely approached the cruiser on the short flight from nearby Selfridge Field, he circled the ship to size up the task before him and then fought off a strong tailwind as the Curtiss Pusher slapped down safely. *Library of Congress*

Left: Seconds after completing his historic landing aboard the USS *Pennsylvania*, pilot Ely exits the aircraft. Observers congratulate him as sailors rush to secure the aircraft, the momentum of which was halted by a system of ropes and sandbags. *National Archives*

This view shows the USS *Pennsylvania*'s wooden flight deck under construction over the ship's stern. When completed, the landing deck that Eugene B. Ely would land on measured 133 feet 7 inches long and 31 feet 6 inches wide. Also visible is Ely's Curtiss Pusher biplane. *Universal History Archive/UIG/Bridgeman Images*

The earliest seaplane carriers of the British Royal Navy were converted steamers that operated in the coastal waters near the English Channel before the outbreak of World War I. They included the *Engadine*, *Empress*, and *Riviera*. In this photo, the HMS *Engadine* is pictured underway in coastal waters off the English shore. The seaplane hangar is clearly visible near the stern. *Zenith Press collection*

continued from page 14

to take advantage of a headwind that would slow Ely's Pusher during the landing, but the winds were unpredictable, and the pilot requested that the ship remain at anchor.

At about 10:45 a.m., Ely took off from Selfridge Field in San Bruno, California, known as the Tanforan Racetrack when it was civilian property. A large crowd gathered on the shore, and curious observers aboard small vessels clustered near the *Pennsylvania* in San Francisco Bay. Despite the unpredictable winds, Ely soon appeared on the horizon. He circled the cruiser once to size up the landing platform and then cut power, reducing speed to roughly forty miles per hour.

As he made his approach, an abrupt tailwind grabbed the Pusher and threatened disaster. The pilot reacted quickly, dropping the nose of the airplane, slapping the deck, and hooking several arresting lines about halfway down the planking. The plane came to a quick stop. The entire flight had taken little more than fifteen minutes.

As Ely climbed from the pilot's seat, his wife, Mabel, greeted him with a breathless "Oh, boy! I knew you could do it!" Captain Pond invited the couple to join him for lunch while the flight deck was cleared of the arresting gear and the Pusher turned around for takeoff. Ely posed for numerous photos, and about an hour after landing he climbed aboard the plane once again and lifted into the air without incident. He landed safely at Selfridge Field. On the ground, Ely smiled and commented to a newspaper reporter, "It was easy enough. I think the trick could be successfully turned nine times out of ten."

Ely had significantly enhanced his reputation as a daring pilot. He tried to interest the navy in hiring him as an aviator, but nothing came of the effort. He continued to fly exhibitions and competitive events until the autumn of 1911. On October 19, he was killed in a crash during a demonstration in Macon, Georgia, unable to pull the plane out of a steep dive; he managed to extricate himself from the wreckage but collapsed

Above: Lt. Charles R. Samson became the first pilot to successfully take off from the deck of a warship that was underway when he took off from the HMS *Hibernia* on May 9, 1913. Samson flew an Improved S.27 No. 38 aircraft across Weymouth Bay and landed at the eastern end of Lodmoor near the village of Preston, England. *© The Keasbury-Gordon Photograph Archive/Alamy*

Left: Great Britain took a leading role in the development of naval aviation prior to World War I. In this photograph, Royal Navy Lt. Arthur M. Longmore takes off his jacket and begins to light a cigarette after landing an aircraft at Montrose, Scotland, in 1913. Longmore made headlines on December 11, 1911, when he landed a Short Improved S.27 No. 38 seaplane in the River Medway in southeast England. Note the Royal Flying Corps patch on the shoulder of the soldier at left. *Zenith Press collection*

A steamship that had operated in the waters off the Isle of Man, the *Ben-my-Chree* was converted into a seaplane carrier for service during World War I. Under the command of Lt. Charles R. Samson, the *Ben-my-Chree* participated in offensive actions in the Mediterranean, where its aircraft reportedly bombed Turkish positions. *Zenith Press collection*

with a broken neck a few minutes later. Onlookers rushed to the crash site and then combed the area for souvenirs, including Ely's personal effects.

Ely was buried in his hometown on his twenty-fifth birthday. In 1933, he was posthumously awarded the Distinguished Flying Cross.

Despite the stirrings of interest in aviation within the US military, the navy's first aircraft carrier, the USS *Langley*, was not completed until the 1920s, converted from the collier USS *Jupiter*, commissioned originally on April 7, 1913. The British Royal Navy took up the torch in developing workable aircraft carrier operations. Established in 1912, the Royal Flying Corps initially exerted control of all military aviation endeavors, including its Naval Wing, authorized in the spring of that year with the issuance of a royal warrant. On July 1, 1914, the Royal Naval Air Service was formally created. Four years later, it was once again combined with the Royal Flying Corps to form the Royal Air Force.

On November 18, 1911, Cmdr. Oliver Schwann was the first British flier to take off from water. Schwann flew a modified Avro Type D biplane powered by a four-cylinder, thirty-five-horsepower Green engine and took off from the sea near Barrow-in-Furness. He purchased the plane with personal funds, covered the fuselage with canvas, and conducted trials with both skids and floats at Cavendish Dock. He repositioned the engine to provide better balance.

Although Schwann had not formally qualified as a pilot, he made numerous attempts to take flight and finally succeeded.

He gunned the engine that fateful day and was surprised with the swiftness of the plane as it bounded along the surface of the water and then vaulted to a height of just over fifteen feet. The hard landing that rather abruptly followed smashed the plane. Nevertheless, Schwann had proven that the takeoff was possible. On December 11, Lt. Arthur M. Longmore of the Royal Navy followed Schwann's heroics by safely landing a Short Improved S.27 No. 38 seaplane in the River Medway in southeast England.

On January 10, 1912, at Sheerness, Royal Navy lieutenant Charles R. Samson piloted an Improved S.27 No. 38 from a one-hundred-foot downward-sloping flight deck constructed above the forward twelve-inch gun mount of the pre-dreadnought battleship HMS *Africa*. Rails were fitted to the flight deck to keep the plane in proper alignment during its run, and crew members of the *Africa* jumped up and down on the wooden apparatus to ensure its sturdiness. Samson needed every inch of the deck before clearing the bow of the battleship, dipping toward the surface of the River Medway, and then steadily climbing.

He reached an altitude of eight hundred feet, circled the battleship several times as the crew cheered wildly, and came dangerously close to the ship's mast during one pass. He touched down safely at a nearby airfield.

In the spring, military and political dignitaries, including King George V, gathered at Weymouth for the 1912 Fleet Review. Four naval aircraft took part in the demonstrations, and on May 9 Samson became the first aviator to take off from the deck of a ship that was underway. The flight deck and supporting structure that had been used successfully aboard the HMS *Africa* in January were transferred to her sister battleship HMS *Hibernia* and affixed at the same location above the forward gun turret.

Samson climbed aboard the Improved S.27 No. 38, warmed up the seventy-horsepower Gnome engine, and hurtled down the flight deck as the *Hibernia* steamed in Weymouth Bay at about ten knots, three miles out of Portland Harbor. This time, he needed less than half the length of the flight deck, leaping into the air after a forty-five-foot run to gain speed. He flew across Weymouth Bay and landed at the eastern end of Lodmoor near the village of Preston. On July 4, with the takeoff equipment transferred again, this time to the battleship HMS *London*, Samson used only twenty-five feet of the flight deck to lift off successfully as the warship steamed into the wind at twelve knots.

Following the triumph at Weymouth, *Flight* magazine, which billed itself as the "Official Organ of the Royal Aero Club of the United Kingdom," reported in its May 18, 1912, edition, "The feats performed by the naval aviators during the King's review of his ships, [*sic*] must have convinced the Naval authorities, if they needed any convincing, of the practical stage attained by aviation, and also that the Navy does not lack officers who are quite competent to rank with any aviators in the world."

By the end of 1912, the potential for flight operations had become a priority for the Royal Navy. Sixteen aircraft were then in service, including eight biplanes and five monoplanes for land operations and three seaplanes. Several seaplane stations were established during the next year, and two aircraft were successfully launched from a runway built forward of the bridge aboard the light cruiser HMS *Hermes*, which was later lost during World War I, torpedoed and sunk by the German submarine *U-27* on October 31, 1914. In October 1912, Samson was promoted to command of the Naval Wing of the Royal Flying Corps.

During World War I, the primary responsibilities of Royal Navy aviators included the air defense of the British Isles, antisubmarine patrols against German U-boats, and security against the bombing raids mounted later in the conflict by German Zeppelins. Seaplane carriers were devised to hoist aircraft into and out of the water, and later some of these were fitted with short flight decks. Seaplanes that were equipped with both floats and retractable wheels took off from these decks, but only on a limited basis.

The first Royal Navy seaplane carriers included the *Engadine*, *Empress*, and *Riviera*, converted steamers that had plied the waters of the English Channel before the war. On December 25, 1914, a dozen seaplanes launched by these carriers mounted the first naval air raid of World War I in Europe, hitting the Zeppelin base at Cuxhaven in Saxony

1914... L'attaque de CUXHAVEN (port allemand, mer du Nord par les hydravions et contre-torpilleurs anglais
1914... The CUXHAVEN action (German port in the north sea) by the English hydroplanes and counter torpedoes

On December 25, 1914, seaplanes of the British Royal Navy's Naval Air Service attacked the German Zeppelin base at Cuxhaven in Saxony. Twelve seaplanes took part in the raid, which was the first attack of its kind in World War I. This rather fanciful interpretation of the event appears to exaggerate the extent of the encounter with airborne Zeppelins participating in the action. *Zenith Press collection*

with disappointing results. In its January 1, 1915, edition, *Flight* magazine trumpeted, "The Cuxhaven raid marks the first employment of the seaplanes of the Naval Air Service in an attack on the enemy's harbours from the sea, and, apart altogether from the results achieved, is an occasion of historical moment. Not only so, but for the first time in history a naval attack has been delivered simultaneously above, on, and from below the surface of the water."

On December 10, 1914, the HMS *Ark Royal*, the first British warship designed and completed as a seaplane carrier, was commissioned. The *Ark Royal* took part in the ill-fated Gallipoli Campaign in the Dardanelles in 1915, as her aircraft were detailed for observation and reconnaissance duties.

Above: The HMS *Ark Royal*, the first warship of the British Royal Navy designed and completed as a seaplane carrier, was commissioned on December 10, 1914. The *Ark Royal* participated in the 1915 campaign in the Dardanelles, and her seaplanes were regularly used for reconnaissance and observation missions. *Library of Congress*

Opposite: In this painting by Wilfred Hardy, Squadron Commander Edwin H. Dunning lands his Sopwith Pup biplane aboard the HMS *Furious* on August 2, 1917. Dunning accomplished the first successful landing of an aircraft aboard a warship that was underway, matching the speed of the *Furious* at twenty-six knots and then cutting the throttle for a rapid descent. Sailors move toward the Sopwith Pup to secure it once Dunning has landed. Tragically, Dunning was killed in an accident five days later. *Wilf (Wilfred) Hardy/Private Collection/© Look and Learn/Bridgeman Images*

Samson was one of the first naval aviators in combat, flying from a land base in the Dardanelles and actually attacking the German submarine *U-21*. On May 14, 1916, he took command of the seaplane carrier *Ben-my-Chree*, a converted passenger steamship that had operated in the waters surrounding the Isle of Man. Samson and his pilots flew Short seaplanes, conducting bombing missions against Turkish positions, and were reported to have actually carried out a torpedo attack against an enemy ship.

Although they provided valuable service, the seaplane carriers were of limited usefulness to the fleet simply because they were unable to keep pace with faster ships, as they were required to stop and start while launching and recovering their planes. The major problem that hindered the seaplane carriers involved the generation of enough airspeed across their flight decks to assist in the launching of wheeled aircraft that were originally land based. The combination of floats equipped with retractable wheels was only partially successful.

The converted ocean liner *Campania* and seaplane carrier *Vindex* conducted milestone operations during the Great War as they demonstrated the capability to work with high-performance land aircraft. When a Sopwith Baby seaplane equipped with dual floats and wheels took off from the

Campania on August 6, 1915, and a Bristol Scout C wheeled biplane took off from the *Vindex* on November 3, using forty-six feet of the flight deck while the carrier steamed at twelve knots, the development and use of carrier air power in wartime made a great leap forward. While operating in the North Sea, Bristol Scouts flying from the *Vindex* attacked the German Zeppelin base at Tønder in southern Denmark and made the first interception of an enemy airship by a carrier-borne plane.

The last and arguably most daunting aspect of carrier air operations involved landing an aircraft on the deck of a ship that was actually underway. In addressing this major issue, the Royal Navy adapted the battlecruiser HMS *Furious* into the first actual aircraft carrier in history. In May 1917, while the *Furious* was under construction, alterations were ordered to remove the forward eighteen-inch gun turret and replace it with a hangar and a flight deck 228 feet in length. The new configuration was workable, but it was not without hazard. Landing planes were required to maneuver around the ship's superstructure in order to come to a halt.

The *Furious* carried an initial complement of six Sopwith Pup fighter planes and four seaplanes led by Squadron Cmdr. Edwin H. Dunning. On August 2, 1917, during trials at the Royal Navy anchorage of Scapa Flow in the Orkney Islands of

Top: The British Royal Navy's HMS *Argus* was the world's first vessel designed and built from the keel up as an aircraft carrier. Plans for such a warship had been considered as early as 1912, and the *Argus* was commissioned on September 16, 1918. Intended for operations in the North Sea, it was not completed until after the Armistice ending World War I was concluded. *Library of Congress*

Above: While the British battlecruiser HMS *Furious* was under construction in May 1916, the Admiralty ordered alterations to remove the forward gun turret and install a hangar and flight deck 288 feet in length. Upon completion, the *Furious* became the first actual aircraft carrier in history. *Zenith Press collection*

Opposite: Three British biplanes sit aligned on the flight deck of the HMS *Furious*, a converted battlecruiser, as crewmen tend to them during operations in World War I. The historic *Furious* served as an aircraft carrier during both world wars and was eventually sold for scrap in 1948. *© Chronicle/Alamy*

Scotland, Dunning took off from the *Furious* in his Sopwith Pup specially equipped with handling straps for deckhands to grab, then matched the ship's cruising speed of twenty-six knots. He flew alongside into a twenty-one-knot headwind and then circled the ship's funnel. He descended rapidly, cut the throttle, and sideslipped near the deck while sailors stretched for the handling straps and muscled the plane to a safe landing.

Five days later, Dunning was again aloft. He duplicated the successful landing and then took off for his second attempt of the day. This time an updraft caught his portside wings and flipped the Sopwith Pup over the edge of the deck as the engine stalled. The plane crashed off the starboard bow, rendering Dunning unconscious. Tragically, he drowned while still strapped in the plane's cockpit.

Dunning's death resulted in the lengthening of the flight deck aboard *Furious* to 284 feet and its repositioning aft of the superstructure. Primitive arresting gear consisting of weighted wires and ropes along with a crash barrier fashioned of ropes were installed. *Furious* and her air component went on to make more history. On July 19, 1918, seven Sopwith Camel fighter planes took off from the carrier's deck and attacked the Zeppelin base at Tønder, destroying two German airships, the *L-54* and *L-60*. During the 1920s, the *Furious* was modified with an upward-sloped flight deck stretching 576 feet long and 92 feet wide, about three-quarters of the ship's full length. The carrier served throughout World War II and was eventually sold for scrap in 1948.

By the waning months of World War I, there was no doubt that the aircraft carrier would play a major role in any future conflict, and the British Admiralty set out to satisfy the requirement for a warship that was specifically designed as an aircraft carrier. The result was the HMS *Argus*, the world's first vessel designed and built as an aircraft carrier.

As early as 1912, the Scottish engineering firm of William Beardmore and Company had proposed to the Admiralty a design for an aircraft carrier with a continuous flight deck

British naval personnel watch the approach of a biplane toward the flight deck of the HMS *Argus,* the first warship in history designed and built as an aircraft carrier. Landings were often more difficult to accomplish than takeoffs, as decks pitched and rolled with the seas. *Windmill/Robert Hunt Library/UIG/Bridgeman Images*

running nearly the entire length of the ship and unobstructed by any superstructure. While the Beardmore plan gained little initial support, the experience with HMS *Furious* validated the need for the new design, and it was revived with vigor.

Getting the aircraft carrier project off the ground presented an early challenge during wartime; however, an immediate solution coincidentally lay in the Beardmore shipyard at Clydebank, West Dunbartonshire, Scotland. The Italian Lloyd Sabaudo passenger line had ordered two vessels from Beardmore in 1914, but the coming of the Great War brought construction of the liner *Conte Rosso* to a halt. The Admiralty purchased the unfinished hull in September 1916, and construction commenced on an aircraft carrier with a full-length flight deck, no superstructure, an enclosed hangar deck where planes could be serviced and readied for operations, and a small pilothouse that could be lowered during flight operations to remove any obstruction. The pilothouse configuration was considered temporary, and during trials in the Firth of Forth the carrier was fitted with a wood and canvas "island" offset from the flight deck for evaluation.

Named after a one hundred-eyed giant of Greek mythology, the 14,550-ton HMS *Argus* was commissioned on September 16, 1918, with a flight deck that stretched 556 feet long, and a complement of 401 personnel. The carrier was powered by four steam turbines delivering twenty thousand shaft horsepower to four propellers that generated a top speed of just over twenty knots. Six 102-millimeter antiaircraft guns were installed, and eighteen Sopwith Cuckoo torpedo bombers were taken aboard.

The Admiralty had hoped the HMS *Argus* might counter a continuing threat to Royal Navy operations in the North Sea that was posed by the German High Seas Fleet. However, its construction was slowed by a severe labor shortage, and by the time the carrier was operational the Armistice had been concluded.

While carrier construction and operations gained momentum, the Royal Navy continued to modify warships to accommodate aircraft. Particular attention was given to wheeled, primarily land-based planes, whose performance was substantially better than that of seaplanes and flying boats. Flight Commander F. J. Rutland made successful takeoffs in unmodified Sopwith Pups from the cruiser *Yarmouth* and the battlecruiser *Repulse* in June and October 1917. When World War I ended, twenty-two light cruisers had been modified with short flight decks for takeoffs, and Royal Navy battleships and battlecruisers were equipped with flight decks that carried

This photograph, taken from near the bridge of the armored cruiser USS *Pennsylvania* at midday on January 18, 1911, captures the moment that the Curtiss Pusher piloted by Eugene B. Ely lifted off from the warship's recently constructed flight deck on his return flight to Selfridge Field, California. Earlier that morning, Ely had taken off from Selfridge Field and successfully executed the first landing by an aircraft on the deck of a ship. His return flight to Selfridge was uneventful. *National Archives*

EXPERIMENTATION WITH PLATFORMS

The earliest flight decks constructed aboard naval vessels consisted of simple wooden planking and were at first specific to takeoff. These wooden ramps were usually quite short due to the low takeoff speeds of the first operational planes. They were built with a downward slope across the bows of warships and situated above a main gun battery. The short length and downward angle combined with the turning of the vessel into the wind assisted the plane in gaining altitude. In time, removable "flying-off" ramps were installed atop the turrets of large vessels such as battleships and battlecruisers to facilitate the launching of scout planes.

Landing aboard a naval vessel, first stationary and then underway, required the installation of arresting gear made of rope or wire weighted with sandbags and then stretched across an upward-sloping flight deck. Early airplanes were not equipped with brakes, so small grappling hooks were installed near the tail to catch the arresting gear while the upward slope was also intended to slow and safely halt a landing plane. With the introduction of the HMS *Argus*, the first purpose-built aircraft carrier, the unobstructed, full-length flight deck became an obvious choice for optimal air operations.

Several key modifications were made to early airplanes, as well, to facilitate their use in naval operations. The first seaplanes were hoisted aboard vessels by cranes that employed a system of ropes and pulleys. These planes were sometimes equipped with floats that also housed retractable wheels that allowed them to roll across a flight deck for takeoff. Wheeled airplanes were sometimes modified with skids for takeoffs or landings aboard ships, and grappling hooks were affixed to the tail sections of airplanes to grasp arresting gear on landing as well. With limited hangar space aboard an aircraft carrier, planes were designed with folding wings. Short Brothers, a British airplane manufacturer, was granted the first patent for a folding wing in 1913. As carrier operations progressed, both single-seat and two-seat planes were routinely deployed.

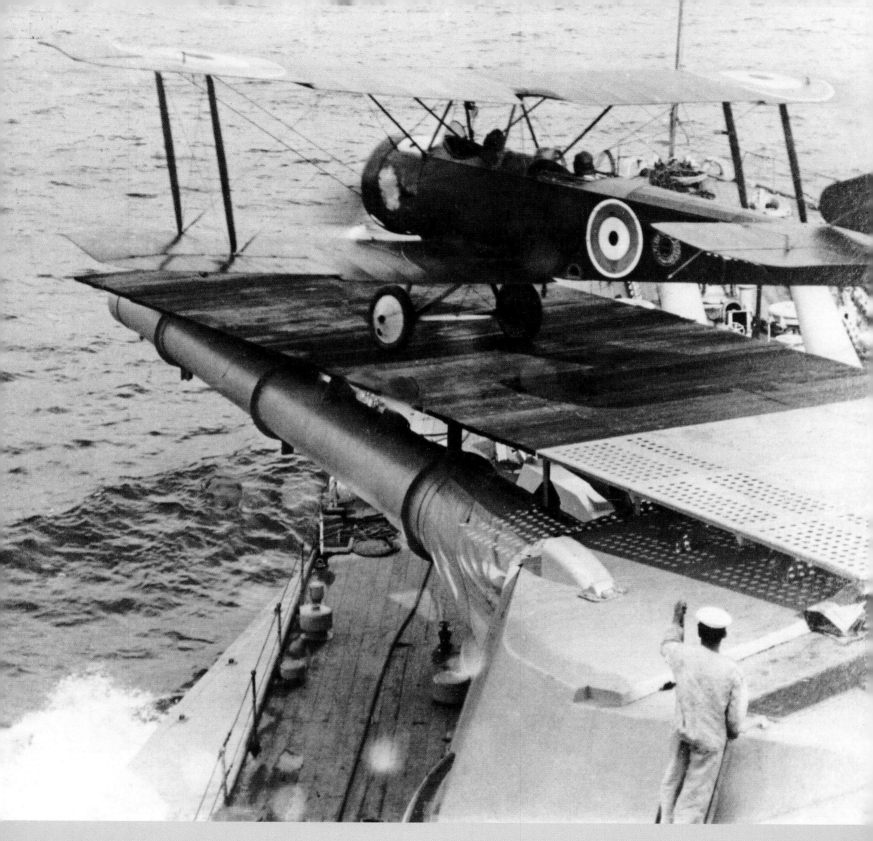

In 1916, a Royal Navy Sopwith 1½ Strutter biplane takes off from the deck of a carrier at speed. This view shows the mounting of the flight deck above the vessel's forward gun turret. By the Great War's end, Royal Navy battleships and battlecruisers were equipped with flight decks that carried two-seat planes atop forward turret flight decks and single-seat fighter planes above rear turrets. *Windmill/Robert Hunt Library/UIG/Bridgeman Images*

This colorful postal issue from 2010 commemorates Henri Fabre's flight a century earlier. Fabre's Hydravion aircraft was powered by a rotary engine that generated fifty horsepower. *Zenith Press collection*

two-seat planes atop forward turret flight decks and single-seat fighter planes above rear turrets. More than one hundred aircraft were being carried aboard British naval vessels.

At the Étang de Berre, a few miles northwest of Marseille on the Mediterranean coast of France, Henri Fabre piloted his Fabre Hydravion seaplane on March 28, 1910, in the first documented takeoff of an airplane from water. The Fabre Hydravion was powered by a seven-cylinder Gnome Omega rotary engine that generated fifty horsepower. Fabre completed four flights that day, the longest covering just over 650 yards. Glenn Curtiss was among numerous other aviators and airplane designers who corresponded with Fabre, who was born on November 29, 1882, and lived to be 101 years old (one of the last surviving twentieth-century aviation pioneers at the time of his death).

Fabre's exploits prompted the French navy to develop the first seaplane carrier in history, the *Foudre*, converted from a minelayer at the French Mediterranean port of Toulon beginning in the winter of 1911. Some observers dispute the claim that the *Foudre* was actually the first vessel of its kind, citing the fact that the HMS *Hermes* was fitted with a temporary flight deck for similar purposes in the spring of 1913. However, the *Foudre*'s service appears to predate the conversion of the *Hermes*. Regardless, its carrier conversion marked the *Foudre*'s fourth incarnation: it had entered service as a torpedo boat tender in 1896, was refitted as a repair ship in 1907, and became a minelayer in 1910.

A flight deck was constructed above the *Foudre*'s bow, and a hangar was placed to the rear of the funnels along with a crane to lift seaplanes from the water upon landing. Facilities were also built to service up to eight seaplanes, including Farman, Nieuport, and Breguet types. Trials and war games were conducted during the summer of 1912, and the 6,713-ton *Foudre* performed well, her seaplanes demonstrating proficiency in reconnaissance.

In November 1913, an improved thirty-three-foot flight deck was installed for use with a Caudron G.3 seaplane, and a successful launch was conducted on May 8, 1914. With the outbreak of World War I, the flight deck was removed and further trials were canceled. The *Foudre* later served as a submarine tender, transport, command ship, and training ship for pilots. The historic vessel was decommissioned in 1921 and sold for scrap.

Although visionary French author and inventor Clément Ader described the modern aircraft carrier with uncanny accuracy in his book *L'Aviation Militaire*, published in 1909, French carrier development stagnated until the 22,500-ton *Béarn*, originally intended as a *Normandie*-class battleship, was completed in 1927 following a five-year conversion program.

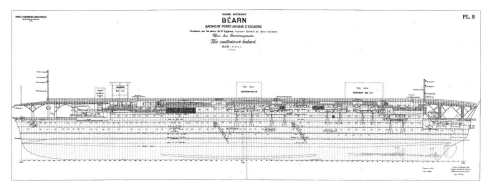

This drawing from the plans for the French aircraft carrier *Béarn* reveals the advances that had been made in aircraft carrier design by the mid-1920s, when the carrier was completed. The *Béarn* displaced 22,500 tons and exhibited a flush deck design with a flight deck that ran the length of the ship.

Zenith Press collection

The carrier entered service eighteen years after the publication of the prophetic *L'Aviation Militaire*.

Ader had written, "An airplane-carrying vessel is indispensable. These vessels will be constructed on a plan very different from what is currently used. First of all the deck will be cleared of all obstacles. It will be flat, as wide as possible without jeopardizing the nautical lines of the hull, and it will look like a landing field. . . . Of necessity, the airplanes will be stowed below decks; they would be solidly anchored to their bases, each in its place, so they would not be affected with the pitching and rolling. Access to this lower deck would be by an elevator sufficiently long and wide to hold an airplane with its wings folded. A large, sliding trap would cover the hole in the deck, and it would have waterproof joints, so that neither rain nor seawater from heavy seas could penetrate below."

According to Ader, landing operations required precision. "The ship will be headed straight into the wind, the stern clear, but a padded bulwark set up forward in case the airplane should run past the stop line."

On the other side of the world, Japanese interest in naval aviation began as early as 1912, after early air enthusiasts had imported a number of European- and American-designed planes and the Imperial Navy formed the Naval Aeronautical Research Committee. Six naval officers were dispatched to the United States and France to purchase seaplanes and learn to fly and service the new aircraft. By 1917, the three major Japanese aircraft manufacturers of the twentieth century—Mitsubishi, Kawasaki, and Nakajima—had begun operations. The first functional aircraft designed in Japan was the Type Yokoshō float biplane, the brainchild of Imperial Japanese Navy Capt. Chikuhei Nakajima and Lt. Kishichi Magoshi, which was completed in 1916.

Nakajima was born on January 1, 1884, in Gunma Prefecture, north of Tokyo. He was commissioned in the navy in 1909 and two years later served as the pilot of Japan's first operational airship. He was sent to the United States for flight training in 1912 and attended the flight school run by Glenn Curtiss in San Diego. He later founded the Nakajima Aircraft Company and completed its first contract with the Japanese military for the delivery of twenty planes.

A naval air installation was built on the coast of Japan near Yokosuka, and on November 2, 1912, a pair of Japanese pilots demonstrated their French Farman and American Curtiss planes there. Within the year, formal training of naval pilots was underway, and in August 1914 the seaplane carrier *Wakamiya Maru* was commissioned. Originally the Russian freighter *Lethington*, the *Wakamiya Maru* was captured during the Russo-Japanese War of 1904–1905 and used as a transport craft before being turned over to the Imperial Navy in 1913. The 7,720-ton vessel was converted to a seaplane carrier the following year and carried four Farman MF.11 "Shorthorn" seaplanes that were raised and lowered to the water by crane.

As World War I escalated in the autumn of 1914, the *Wakamiya Maru* operated against the German stronghold of Tsingtao on the Chinese mainland. Her complement of seaplanes attacked numerous targets, including the German gunboat *Jaguar* and the Austro-Hungarian cruiser *Kaiserin Elisabeth*. These were the world's first documented air attacks launched from the sea.

Two officers of the British Royal Navy observed the Japanese air operations off Tsingtao and reported, "Daily reconnaissances, weather permitting, were made by the Japanese seaplanes, working from the seaplane mother ship. They continued to bring valuable information throughout the siege. The mother ship was fitted with a couple of derricks for hoisting them in and out. During these reconnaissances they were constantly fired at by the German guns mostly with shrapnel, but were never hit. The Japanese airmen usually carried bombs for dropping on the enemy positions."

Altogether, the *Wakamiya Maru* aircraft launched fifty attacks against German positions around Tsingtao and dropped nearly two hundred bombs. They were reported to have sunk a German minelayer as well. In the spring of 1920, the *Wakamiya Maru* was converted to an aircraft carrier, and the first successful Japanese takeoff from a carrier deck was accomplished in June of that year.

The Imperial Japanese Navy established its first two air groups, or kōkūtai, before the end of World War I. These were established at Yokosuka in April 1916 and Sasebo in March 1918.

Despite the aeronautical accomplishments of men such as Henri Fabre and the prophetic writings of author and inventor Clément Ader, the development of a French aircraft carrier was delayed until the *Béarn* was planned and completed in the mid-1920s. The *Béarn* was commissioned after a five-year conversion program that transformed the hull of a *Normandie*-class battleship into an aircraft carrier. *Zenith Press collection*

RESHAPING NAVAL WARFARE

During the final year of World War I, the British Royal Navy committed to a future that involved the aircraft carrier. With the construction and eventual deployment of the HMS *Argus* after the Armistice, the British acknowledged two things: their wartime experience during the Battle of Jutland revealed that seaborne reconnaissance was inadequate during the run-up to a major surface engagement, and aircraft flying from the decks of carriers could provide far better real-time intelligence on enemy warship deployments.

Further, the British and Japanese had also demonstrated the offensive capability of carrier-borne aircraft with their respective raids on German Zeppelin

A Fairey Flycatcher fighter plane cruises above the HMS *Eagle*, one of two Royal Navy carriers under construction prior to the end of World War I. The *Eagle* was converted from the hull of a dreadnought battleship and participated in flight operations off the coast of Sicily in 1920 that helped to shape Royal Navy air operations doctrine and procedures. *Royal Air Force Museum/Getty Images*

bases along the North Sea and fortifications and shipping at Tsingtao. The further development of the aircraft carrier, however, was confronted by the stark realities of the postwar world. The financial burden of World War I left most European nations in heavy debt, while many senior commanders of the world's great navies had been "raised" during the dreadnought era and remained firmly convinced that nothing on the high seas would ever eclipse the awesome power of the battleship. These "battleship factions" argued forcefully against the spending of precious resources on the new aircraft carrier.

Perhaps the most daunting obstacle of all was the war weariness deeply felt across the globe during the 1920s and 1930s. The human tragedy of the Great War gave rise to a wave of pacifism and a widespread call for disarmament. In the United States, for example, concern that the nation had become embroiled in a European war led to an isolationist sentiment that was a significant factor in American foreign policy until the Japanese attack on Pearl Harbor in 1941.

During the early years of the twentieth century, Great Britain maintained the largest navy in the world, safeguarding its far-flung empire and serving as the primary instrument of national security. The United States and Japan, both allies of Britain during World War I, also constructed powerful navies during the period. Japan patterned its naval organization after the British Royal Navy and purchased warships built in British shipyards. President Woodrow Wilson, meanwhile, recognized the need for a naval presence that would protect the nation on both its Atlantic and Pacific coasts and defend American territorial possessions.

In 1916, Wilson announced a planned three-year expansion of the two-ocean US Navy that included the construction of numerous battleships, increasing its total number to fifty. Although opposition developed in Congress and the American public's response was mixed, the construction of six new battleships and six battlecruisers commenced. Britain and Japan also began significant expansions of their fleets.

The burgeoning arms race brought the world's major naval powers to the negotiating table in Washington, D.C.,

Smoke trails from the funnel of the HMS *Hermes* as the ship generates power to get underway. This photograph was taken off the coast of Yantai, China, in 1931. About half the size of the *Eagle*, *Hermes* was the first British aircraft carrier designed and built from the keel up and displaced just over eleven thousand tons. *National Naval Aviation Museum/Robert L. Lawson Photograph Collection/1996.488.037.035*

Along with the HMS *Eagle*, the *Hermes* was under construction prior to the end of World War I. The *Hermes*, based on an improved seaplane carrier design, was launched in September 1919 and commissioned in July 1923, after the flight trials conducted aboard *Eagle* resulted in two reconfigurations while the carrier was under construction. This view of the *Hermes* from off its port quarter was taken in 1937. *Zenith Press collection*

in November 1921. Ironically, the Washington Naval Arms Limitation Conference, intended to curb the threat of war and the cost of a naval arms race, fueled the development of the aircraft carrier, the most offensively capable warship to ever set sail. Perhaps this was an unintended consequence. However, the result of the treaty, concluded by the United States, Great Britain, Japan, France, and Italy on February 6, 1922, cannot be denied.

In the midst of its massive naval buildup, the United States expressed a willingness to consign a percentage of its naval tonnage then under construction to the scrapyard in exchange for limitations on the types and tonnage that each signatory would be authorized to complete. The famous tonnage ratio of 5:5:3 for aircraft carriers and battleships was agreed for

the United States, Great Britain, and Japan, respectively, while France and Italy each were allowed to maintain a 1.75 comparative tonnage ratio. Battleships were restricted to no more than thirty-five thousand tons, and a ten-year moratorium on the construction of new capital ships, namely battleships and battlecruisers, was affirmed.

At the time the Washington treaty was concluded, the US Navy had a pair of battlecruisers, the *Lexington* and the *Saratoga*, under construction. The treaty provided for a maximum of 135,000 total US aircraft carrier tonnage, and the two were converted to carriers even though they were 33,000-ton ships, exceeding the allowable tonnage for individual carriers that had been set at 27,000.

During the early 1920s, the converted battlecruiser HMS *Furious* was modified with an island, a flight deck that stretched the entire length of the ship, and a hangar that could accommodate ten aircraft. One of the earliest aircraft carriers in service with the Royal Navy, the *Furious* was already aging by the time the modernization occurred. *Library of Congress*

By the early 1920s, the world's three major naval powers had begun to augment their naval aviation efforts, and the most tangible evidence of this was the conversion and construction of aircraft carriers. At any given time no fewer than six aircraft carriers were either in service or under construction by the middle of the decade.

When the Armistice was signed, the 14,550-ton *Argus* was operational with the British Royal Navy. Two other carriers, the *Eagle* and the *Hermes*, were under construction. The *Eagle* was converted from the hull of a dreadnought-era battleship, while the *Hermes* was the first British carrier designed and built from the keel up.

The 22,200-ton HMS *Eagle* was launched on June 6, 1918, and commissioned on April 13, 1920. Sir E. H. Tennyson d'Eyncourt, the Royal Navy's director of naval construction, spearheaded the redesign of the ship into an aircraft carrier with a flight deck extending the full 670-foot length of the hull. No island or masts were built above the level of the flight deck, and thirty-two Yarrow tube boilers were installed to make steam for four Parsons geared turbines that generated fifty thousand shaft horsepower and a top speed of twenty-four knots. Nine six-inch guns were mounted for protection against enemy surface vessels, and a quartet of four-inch antiaircraft guns was installed.

Practical experience, including the *Eagle*'s flight trials in the Mediterranean Sea off the coast of Sicily and lessons from the air operations aboard *Argus*, influenced a redesign of the *Eagle*

that began in the autumn of 1920 and required more than three years to complete. An island was constructed on the starboard side of the flight deck to facilitate air operations and navigation, and a second funnel was added. A pair of masts was attached in line atop the island, with a gunnery fire control station forward. At various times, and depending on the types taken aboard, the *Eagle* could carry from twenty-one to thirty aircraft.

The HMS *Hermes* was launched on September 11, 1919, and commissioned on July 7, 1923. Smaller than the *Eagle*, the *Hermes* was 598 feet long, and her flight deck stretched 570 feet. The carrier displaced 11,020 tons. Six water-tube boilers and two geared steam turbines produced forty thousand shaft horsepower and a top speed of twenty-five knots. Six single-mount 5.5-inch guns and three four-inch antiaircraft guns protected the ship, which carried a complement of fifteen to twenty aircraft.

For the *Hermes*, d'Eyncourt refined a seaplane carrier design that had been proposed in 1916 by engineers John Biles and Gerard Holmes. An ingenious retractable slipway was designed to accommodate seaplanes, and a pair of islands, one on each side of the flight deck, would provide space for control of air operations and navigation. A large net could be extended between the islands to halt careening aircraft.

A delay in the construction of the *Hermes* occurred while the *Eagle* and *Argus* conducted their influential flight trials, and the *Hermes* was redesigned in two stages during 1920 and 1921. The seaplane slipway was discarded, a single island

DEVELOPING CARRIER DOCTRINE

Early aircraft carrier doctrine developed with the realization that the warship was capable of decisive offensive action. The fleet carriers of the US Navy demonstrated this on more than one occasion during war games, or fleet problems, in the late 1920s and early 1930s. Without doubt, the successful "attack" launched by the carriers *Saratoga* and *Lexington* during Grand Joint Exercise No. 4 against Pearl Harbor on February 7, 1932, proved that such an operation was not only feasible but potentially crippling for the US Pacific Fleet.

The Japanese certainly took note of the event, which emboldened them to plan and launch the Pearl Harbor attack nearly a decade later. In doing so, the Imperial Japanese Navy unveiled the Kidō Butai, its tactical aircraft carrier battle group consisting of the fleet carriers *Akagi*, *Kaga*, *Sōryū*, *Hiryū*, *Shōkaku*, and *Zuikaku*. Admiral Isoroku Yamamoto, commander-in-chief of the Combined Fleet, realized that the concentrated air power of the carrier battle group could strike a decisive blow against an enemy's navy across the expanse of the Pacific Ocean, and the concept of the battle group survives today.

Below: The obsolete battleship USS *Indiana* lies half submerged in the waters of Chesapeake Bay after being used as a target ship during demonstrations of aerial bombing conducted by the US Navy on November 1, 1920. The tests utilized dummy bombs and explosives placed aboard the ship and detonated at the locations where bombs actually hit. The navy authorized the tests in response to the assertion of controversial General Billy Mitchell that planes of his US Army Air Service were capable of sinking any battleship then afloat. *National Archives*

Inset: Admiral Isoroku Yamamoto, commander-in-chief of the Imperial Japanese Navy's Combined Fleet, was a formidable advocate of naval air power and earned his pilot's wings at an advanced age. Yamamoto grasped the potential of the carrier battle group, a concept that remains viable in warfare today. He opposed going to war with the United States but became the primary architect of the attack on Pearl Harbor on December 7, 1941. *Public domain*

The HMS *Courageous* began its naval career as a battlecruiser. After service during World War I, the *Courageous* and her sister HMS *Glorious* were converted to aircraft carriers under the terms of the Washington Naval Treaty of 1922. The full-length photo reveals the *Courageous's* clean lines and large funnel. Well over twice the size of the HMS *Hermes*, the carriers of the *Courageous* class were evidence that the Admiralty acknowledged the growing importance of such ships. *Royal Navy photo*

was placed starboard of the flight deck, two elevators that transported aircraft from the hangar deck to the flight deck were repositioned, and the flight deck was made flush with the bow.

By the mid-1920s, serious concerns about the future viability of the battlecruiser concept and the conclusion of the Washington Naval Treaty prompted the Admiralty to evaluate the future of its warships then in service. By 1925, the hybrid battlecruiser-carrier HMS *Furious* was modified with a full-length flight deck, an island, and a hangar that could accommodate ten aircraft.

Two other battlecruisers, the HMS *Courageous* and HMS *Glorious*, were commissioned in 1917, and some issues arose concerning significant stress on the hull during sea trials. Nevertheless, both saw action during World War I. Under the terms of the Washington Naval Treaty, the Royal Navy was allowed to convert just over sixty-seven thousand tons of existing warships to aircraft carriers, and work began on both the *Courageous* and the *Glorious* in 1924 at the Royal

Dockyards in Devonport. Both refits were completed by 1930. With the conversions, the Admiralty acknowledged that the carrier was reshaping the future of naval warfare.

The two ships of the new *Courageous* class were fitted with eighteen Yarrow boilers and four Parsons steam turbines that delivered ninety thousand shaft horsepower and a top speed of thirty knots. A 550-foot hangar with a sixteen-foot ceiling was built atop the hull, while a short flying-off deck was installed below the main flight deck at hangar level. This was later discarded as carrier aircraft with greater thrust were developed. The *Glorious* displaced slightly greater tonnage than the *Courageous* at 25,370 and 24,600, respectively—each well over twice the displacement of the HMS *Hermes*.

Each converted carrier was home to a complement of up to forty-eight aircraft, including the Blackburn Dart torpedo bomber, the Fairey Flycatcher fighter, and the Fairey III reconnaissance plane. During the 1930s, a new generation of carrier-borne aircraft was taken aboard, including the Hawker

Above: The second aircraft carrier of the *Courageous* class, the HMS *Glorious* was also a converted battlecruiser. Work on the conversion began in 1924 at the Royal Dockyards in Devonport and was completed by 1930. The *Glorious* was slightly larger than the *Courageous* and displaced more than twenty-five thousand tons. *Royal Navy photo*

Following pages: On September 17, 1939, two weeks after Great Britain went to war with Nazi Germany, the HMS *Courageous* was on patrol off the coast of Ireland. Two torpedoes from the German submarine *U-29* struck the port side of the carrier, which sank in twenty minutes with the loss of five hundred lives. This dramatic artist's rendering depicts the final moments of the *Courageous* before the carrier plunged to the bottom of the Atlantic. *Library of Congress*

Above: A crewman aboard the Royal Navy aircraft carrier HMS *Illustrious* guides an approaching aircraft as it attempts to land on the warship's flight deck. The crewman is utilizing an innovative apparatus of battery-powered lights to direct the pilot safely aboard the carrier. *Hulton Archive/Getty Images*

Opposite: Construction proceeds on the Royal Navy aircraft carrier HMS *Illustrious,* which was laid down at the Vickers Armstrong Yards at Barrow on April 27, 1937, and commissioned on May 25, 1940. Great Britain was already at war with Nazi Germany by the time the *Illustrious* entered service, and the event was delayed to permit the installation of new radar. *David Savill/Getty Images*

Nimrod and Osprey fighters and the Fairey Swordfish biplane torpedo bomber.

While the threat of war with Nazi Germany increased, the Royal Navy continued to construct aircraft carriers of more practical designs. Under their programs of 1936, 1937, and 1938, the carriers of the *Illustrious* and *Implacable* classes were ordered. The HMS *Illustrious* was laid down on April 27, 1937, at the Vickers Armstrong yards at Barrow and commissioned on May 25, 1940, when Great Britain was already at war. The completion of the HMS *Illustrious* was delayed to permit the installation of Type 79 radar to warn of approaching aircraft. The carrier was the first to mount this key defensive apparatus.

The *Illustrious* class also included the HMS *Formidable* and HMS *Victorious,* also laid down in the spring of 1937

—the *Formidable* at Harland and Wolff Ltd. in Belfast, Northern Ireland, and the *Victorious* at Vickers-Armstrongs in Wallsend. Built with a starboard island and single funnel, each of the carriers displaced 23,369 standard tons, and their three Admiralty boilers and Parsons geared steam turbines generated 111,000 shaft horsepower and a top speed of thirty-one knots. The *Illustrious* was 753 feet long with a flight deck of 620 feet, while flight decks of 650 feet were installed on the *Formidable* and *Victorious.* A single armored hangar was serviced by a pair of elevators that transported aircraft to the flight deck above. Antiaircraft defenses were modified during the war years and included a mixture of two-pounder, forty-millimeter Bofors, and twenty-millimeter Oerlikon guns.

The HMS *Indefatigable* is launched by the John Brown & Co. of Clydebank, Scotland, in December 1943. The *Indefatigable* continued the British design philosophy of two hangars and armor protection, which reduced its aircraft capacity to forty-eight planes. © *War Archive/Alamy*

The *Illustrious* class was designed under the watchful eye of Adm. Sir Reginald Henderson, third sea lord and controller of the navy, responsible for materiel and procurement. Henderson saw the coming of war with Germany and believed that the carriers were likely to be operating in the confines of the North Sea, the Mediterranean Sea, and the English Channel, where they would be vulnerable to attacks from enemy aircraft. In response, the single hangar was armored both to protect the ship and its aircraft while sustaining air operations in the

event of damage to the vessel. The tradeoff was an aircraft complement of thirty-six planes, roughly half that of earlier carriers without such armored protection above the waterline.

By 1937, however, concerns surrounding the low number of aircraft aboard the *Illustrious*-class carriers prompted a redesign. The HMS *Indomitable* retained the armored flight deck of the *Illustrious* class, but a second hangar was built above the single hangar in the original design, raising the number of planes aboard to forty-eight. To accommodate the second hangar, the level of the flight deck was raised fourteen feet while a portion of the lower hangar was converted to maintenance space for the additional planes.

The *Indomitable* has alternately been grouped with the *Illustrious* class or with the last of the Royal Navy carriers laid down with the approach of World War II in 1939. These were the HMS *Implacable* and HMS *Indefatigable*. These carriers are referred to either as the *Implacable* class or the modified *Illustrious* class. The *Implacable* was laid down in February 1939 and constructed by Fairfield Shipbuilders of Govan, Glasgow, in Scotland. Three Admiralty boilers and Parsons geared steam turbines delivered 148,000 shaft horsepower and a top speed of thirty-two and one-half knots. The *Indefatigable* was laid

down on November 3, 1942, and constructed by John Brown and Company of Clydebank, Scotland.

Construction of the *Implacable*-class carriers was suspended early in World War II as priority was given to destroyers, corvettes, and other small warships to provide escorts for transatlantic convoys. The *Implacable* was finally launched in December 1942, and the *Indefatigable* a year later. Like their immediate predecessor, these carriers were built with two hangars, and armor protection was reduced to accommodate forty-eight planes below decks. Like their American counterparts, the British introduced the concept of the deck park, allowing planes to be carried on the flight deck and increasing the air complement to eighty-one.

The HMS *Ark Royal* was photographed at Portsmouth in late 1938 for the *Illustrated London News*. The most famous of the Royal Navy's aircraft carriers designed and commissioned prior to World War II, the *Ark Royal* displaced twenty-two thousand tons and was the only ship built to its particular design. *De Agostini Picture Library/A. Dagli Orti/Bridgeman Images*

The most famous of the Royal Navy aircraft carriers designed prior to World War II was HMS *Ark Royal*, the second carrier to bear the name. The first was a 7,750-ton seaplane carrier that was completed in 1914 and served during World War I. The second *Ark Royal* was designed in 1934 to comply with the tonnage restrictions of the Washington Naval Treaty. Displacing twenty-two thousand standard tons, the carrier was laid down in September 1935 and built by Cammell Laird and Company on the banks of the River Mersey.

Although the *Ark Royal* was the only ship constructed to its particular design, she was the first with the hangar and flight deck configured as integral components of the hull instead of being added later or adapted to the superstructure. The genesis of the famed carrier began with the Admiralty's decision to undertake a ten-year construction program in 1923; however, economic hardships that followed World War I resulted in a lengthy postponement.

While the development of the Fleet Air Arm was a principal component of the 1923 mandate, only one aircraft carrier was included. Still, the charge for Sir Arthur Johns, then the Royal Navy's director of naval construction, was to employ the latest technology available. Beginning in 1930, Johns did so. He was intent on maximizing the number of aircraft that could be carried, employing the steam catapult and arresting lines to speed the processes of takeoff and landing, and maximizing the utilization of space.

The *Ark Royal* was built with two hangars, one above the other, serviced by three elevators. Originally, the carrier could accommodate up to seventy-two aircraft, but this number was reduced to around fifty as the size and weight of the planes increased. Unlike the later *Illustrious*-class carriers, the *Ark Royal*'s hangars were not completely armored and were protected primarily along the outer edge by the belt armor that was integral to the ship's hull. The flight deck of the *Ark Royal* was eight hundred feet long, substantially longer than those of the *Illustrious*-class carriers, and extended more than one hundred feet beyond the length of the keel. It was also a dizzying sixty-six feet above the waterline.

The *Ark Royal* was powered by six Admiralty boilers and three Parsons turbines, which produced a top speed of thirty-one knots. On the eve of World War II, the carrier's air complement included as many as six squadrons equipped with

Pictured in 1913 as an accompanying tugboat nudges it to its moorings, the collier *Jupiter* was destined to play a key role in the US Navy's development of aircraft carriers. Conversion of the collier to an aircraft carrier was authorized in the summer of 1919, and work began the following spring at the Norfolk Navy Yard. The converted warship was renamed the USS *Langley*. *US Navy photo*

Taken in 1923, this remarkable image depicts an aircraft landing on the deck of the USS *Langley* while spectators admire the spectacle from a waterside park. The *Langley* was the first aircraft carrier commissioned into the US Navy, and this photograph reveals why the vessel was nicknamed the "Covered Wagon." The *Langley* displaced 11,500 tons and carried up to thirty-six aircraft. By the mid-1930s, the carrier was obsolete and underwent a conversion as a seaplane tender. *Library of Congress*

the Blackburn Skua, a dive-bomber and fighter; the Blackburn Roc fighter; and the Fairey Swordfish torpedo bomber. The *Ark Royal* was launched on April 13, 1937, and entered service the following December. During her brief career, Royal Navy aircraft carrier tactics and operating procedures were evaluated and improved.

The senior commanders of the US Navy were involved in pioneering naval aviation developments during the interwar years, in some cases as witnesses and in others as active participants. Although they helped to plan the demonstration, senior naval officers were skeptical both before and after a

historic attack led by Gen. Billy Mitchell against stationary ships anchored off Cape Hatteras, North Carolina.

Mitchell sought to prove that surface vessels, particularly battleships, were vulnerable to air attack. He was only partially successful, and his zeal eventually resulted in a court-martial. However, even the admirals of the strong "battleship faction" in the US Navy had to grudgingly acknowledge that air power would become a factor in future naval operations—if only to provide reconnaissance.

During the late 1920s and early 1930s, the carriers *Lexington* and *Saratoga* were the largest and fastest ships of

In early 1922, naval experts appeared before the House Naval Affairs Committee with models used to demonstrate the feasibility of converting battlecruisers already under construction into aircraft carriers. The group shown, from left to right, comprises Adm. David W. Taylor; Adm. William A. Moffett, chief bureau of aeronautics; Rep. Frederick C. Hicks (NY); Rep. Clark Burdick (RI); Rep. Philip D. Swing (CA); and Adm. John K. Robison, engineer in chief of the Bureau of Engineering. *National Naval Aviation Museum/1996.488.012.001*

their type in the world. During fleet problems, or war games, the carriers were used in an offensive role, making successful simulated strikes on the Panama Canal and Pearl Harbor. Perhaps, then, the Americans were the first to really grasp the offensive potential of the purpose-built aircraft carrier fully integrated into fleet operations. In August 1921, the navy established its Bureau of Aeronautics, and subsequently an assistant secretary of the navy was designated to oversee aviation development.

US carrier design efforts dated to the closing months of World War I. Then, in the summer of 1919, the conversion of the collier USS *Jupiter* was authorized. By the following spring work had begun at the Norfolk Navy Yard in Virginia, including the elimination of the collier's superstructure with the relocation of its two funnels to the portside aft along the flight deck that ran the length of the 542-foot hull and the installation of a single elevator. Three boilers and a General Electric turbo-electric system generated 7,200 shaft horsepower and a top speed of fifteen and one-half knots. Renamed the USS *Langley* in honor of Samuel P. Langley, a scientist, engineer, and aviation enthusiast, the carrier was commissioned on April 7, 1922.

Designated CV-1, with C denoting "carrier" and V indicating the use of aircraft that were "heavier than air," the *Langley* was nicknamed the "Covered Wagon." The carrier displaced 11,500 tons and accommodated up to thirty-six aircraft, although its short length allowed only relatively slow biplanes such as the Vought VE-7 fighter to take off and land. Its capabilities were primitive, but the vessel served as a platform for the development of early carrier-borne aircraft operations in the US Navy. Among the most significant of these was the introduction of tailhooks on planes that were intended to grasp cables stretched across the flight deck and connected to a braking system. By the mid-1930s, the *Langley* was obsolescent, and the ship was converted to a seaplane tender at the Mare Island Navy Yard near San Francisco.

The construction of the US Navy's first fleet carriers, the *Lexington* and *Saratoga*, began in the early 1920s, and after a brief suspension of work both were reauthorized from battlecruisers to aircraft carriers on July 1, 1922. The *Saratoga* was launched in April 1925, the *Lexington* six months later, and the ships were commissioned within a month of one another: the *Saratoga* in November 1927 and the *Lexington* in December. The carriers' unarmored flight decks were 866 feet long, and each was equipped with a pair of elevators to transport planes to and from the immense 450-foot, two-story hangar deck a level below. An island with a large single funnel was offset to the starboard side. Each vessel was powered by sixteen boilers and General Electric turbo-electric systems that produced 180,000 shaft horsepower and a top speed of just over thirty-three knots.

The two *Lexington*-class carriers were originally intended to carry seventy-eight aircraft, but with the introduction of a deck park the number increased to about ninety. The initial types included the Grumman F2F and Boeing F4B biplane fighters, the Vought SBU Corsair and Great Lakes BGH biplane dive-bombers, and other types, which gave way to single-seat monoplanes such as the Grumman F4F Wildcat, the Douglas SBD Dauntless dive-bomber and TBD Devastator torpedo bomber, and the Vought SB2U Vindicator dive-bomber that were introduced in the mid-1930s. Engineer Carl Norden, famous for the invention of a top-secret bombsight that bears his name, designed the initial arrestor gear and catapult equipment. Eight-inch gun batteries were removed in 1942, and the antiaircraft capability included 1.1-inch guns in quadruple mounts, twenty-millimeter Oerlikon cannon, .50-caliber machine guns, and, in the case of the *Saratoga*, forty-millimeter Bofors guns.

The first US Navy aircraft carrier designed and built as such from the keel up was the USS *Ranger*, ordered under the terms of the "cruiser bill" sponsored by the administration of President Calvin Coolidge after his advocacy of continued tonnage limitations achieved little during the Geneva Naval Conference of 1927. Coolidge subsequently believed that US naval strength should equal that of the British Royal Navy, and the provisions of the cruiser bill allowed for construction of a single aircraft carrier.

Above: The US Navy fleet carrier *Saratoga* enters dry dock in Puget Sound, Washington, as crewmen and dockworkers congregate along the deck and the surrounding yard. The *Saratoga* was launched in April 1925 and commissioned in November 1927. Originally intended to accommodate seventy-eight aircraft, both the *Saratoga* and *Lexington* were able to handle ninety due to the introduction of the deck park. *National Archives*

This page and following: Letters written by sailors to friends and family while in port or at sea were often sent in colorful and richly illustrated envelopes. This sampling shows several letters postmarked aboard the USS *Ranger* and USS *Saratoga* between 1935 and 1940. *Zenith Press collection*

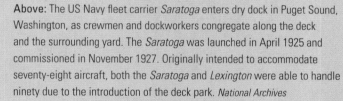

Laid down on September 26, 1931, at Newport News Shipbuilding in Virginia, the *Ranger* was launched on February 25, 1933, and commissioned on June 4, 1934. Displacing only 14,500 standard tons, the *Ranger* was less than half the size of the larger fleet carriers and could not be classified as such. Her flight deck was 769 feet long, extending nearly 40 feet beyond the hull. Six boilers and a pair of steam turbines produced 53,500 shaft horsepower and a top speed of slightly more than twenty-nine knots.

Although the *Ranger* could carry eighty-six planes, nearly as many as its larger contemporaries, she was lightly armored and her speed was mediocre at best. A small island was added to an originally flush deck design, and a trio of funnels was swung away from the superstructure during flight operations to clear the deck of any potential obstacles. The *Ranger* also tended to roll in heavy seas, restricting flight operations in open water.

In the midst of the Great Depression, Americans elected Franklin D. Roosevelt president of the United States. A former assistant secretary of the navy, Roosevelt saw naval expansion not only as a prudent defense measure but also as a creator of jobs. Congressional action in 1934 authorized a multiyear program of naval construction that included aircraft carriers. The ensuing *Yorktown*-class aircraft carriers, the USS *Yorktown* and USS *Enterprise*, were designed with the practical benefit of the lessons learned from their predecessors.

Both products of Newport News Shipbuilding, the *Yorktown* was laid down on May 21, 1934, launched on April 4, 1936, and commissioned on September 30, 1937, while the *Enterprise* was laid down on July 16, 1934, launched on October 3, 1936, and commissioned on May 12, 1938. These carriers were 769 feet long with two hangars on the same level serviced by three elevators. Nine Babcock and Wilcox boilers fed four Parsons geared steam turbines that produced 120,000 shaft horsepower and a top speed of thirty-two and one-half knots. Antiaircraft defenses comprised single-mount eight-inch guns, quad-mounted 1.1-inch weapons, .50-caliber machines guns, and, later, twenty-millimeter Oerlikon cannons. The complement of aircraft included up to ninety planes.

The efficient design of the *Yorktown*-class carriers proved to be the shape of things to come with the legendary wartime *Essex* class that soon followed.

HANDLING AIRCRAFT

Aircraft carrier designs and shipboard routines for handling takeoffs, landings, storage, and servicing of planes influenced one another during the early decades of carrier deployment. Immediate problems, such as the capacity to carry a complement of aircraft that was large enough to accomplish a given mission, resulted in the introduction of aircraft with folding wings and the idea of the deck park. Conversely, the development of larger and more powerful aircraft contributed to the demise of multiple short flight decks, since these were no longer practical in launching and recovery.

The security of armored hangars and flight decks was either embraced or discarded. British carriers, for example, were typically armored, reducing the number of aircraft carried. In contrast, the flight decks of US carriers were not armored in favor of carrying more planes.

Carrier designs influenced the aircraft handling routine. The hangars of US carriers were easily ventilated with the opening of screens to allow exhaust fumes and gasoline vapors to escape. Therefore, engines could be warmed up in the hangar and aircraft elevated to the flight deck, and then the launch sequence could be rapidly executed. Japanese hangars were enclosed, preventing the engines of planes from being warmed up below decks. Aboard Japanese carriers, the planes were brought to the flight deck and then warmed up, appreciably lengthening the time required to launch a large air strike.

On July 1, 1922, two unfinished US Navy battlecruisers were authorized for reclassification as aircraft carriers. The USS *Lexington* and USS *Saratoga* thus became the navy's first fleet carriers and were distinctive and easily identifiable with their large single funnels. This aerial view also illustrates how the development of larger and more powerful aircraft contributed to the demise of multiple short flight decks. *National Archives*

Admiral James M. Russell, a navy pilot who had served aboard the *Langley*, *Lexington*, *Saratoga*, and *Ranger*, was assigned to the *Yorktown* as the carrier was under construction. He knew the shortcomings of the earlier carriers firsthand and gave advice liberally on how to improve the new design—right down to the pilots' ready rooms.

"So, while I was in Newport News fitting out the *Yorktown*, we fought for a lot of things," Russell wrote later. "We put reclining chairs in the ready rooms, all facing in one direction with a blackboard, and a teletype information system that could be operated from a central point, air plot. . . . Air conditioning came in too, and if you were sitting for long hours in a flight suit you would appreciate that very much, particularly in the tropics. So we did a lot of these things in the *Yorktown*, and then later in her sister ship the *Enterprise*."

The US Navy added one more carrier under the terms of the Washington Naval Treaty, the 14,700-ton USS *Wasp*, laid down on April 1, 1936, launched three years later, and commissioned on April 25, 1940. The *Wasp* was built at the Fore River Shipyard in Quincy, Massachusetts, with the intent to maximize its complement of aircraft while economizing significantly on tonnage. The result was an inadequate powerplant with only seventy thousand shaft horsepower delivered by six boilers and two Parsons steam turbines. Its top speed of twenty-nine and one-half knots was a handicap at sea, and the mistakes made with the *Ranger* design were repeated to an extent in the *Wasp*. One notable design innovation that was replicated with the *Essex*-class fleet carriers was the location of an elevator at the edge of the flight deck to ease the handling of aircraft.

The last US Navy fleet aircraft carrier commissioned before the nation was plunged into World War II was the USS *Hornet*, built along the *Yorktown*-class template, although slightly larger at twenty thousand tons and incorporating a few other alterations. Hornet was laid down at Newport News on September 25, 1939, launched on December 14, 1940, and commissioned on October 20, 1941.

The USS *Enterprise* was the second warship of the *Yorktown* class. The *Enterprise* was launched on October 3, 1936, and commissioned on May 12, 1938. The two carriers of the *Yorktown* class were authorized by Congress in the midst of the Great Depression, and incorporated many of the lessons learned from the designs of their predecessors. They became arguably the most famous aircraft carriers of the US Navy during World War II. *John S. Smith/Private Collection/© Look and Learn/Bridgeman Images*

Pilots sit in the ready room aboard the USS *Enterprise* months before the United States entered World War II. The *Enterprise* and its sister, the USS *Yorktown*, had an aircraft capacity of up to ninety planes, and each was capable of a top speed of more than thirty-two knots. *Peter Stackpole/Getty Images*

Across the Pacific, the Imperial Japanese Navy commissioned the world's first warship designed and built as an aircraft carrier from the keel up. The *Hōshō* was laid down in December 1920, launched eleven months later, and commissioned on December 27, 1922, seven months before the British Royal Navy's HMS *Hermes*. The *Hōshō* was small, displacing only 7,400 tons, and powered by eight Kampon Ro-Gō boilers with two Kampon geared steam turbines generating thirty thousand shaft horsepower and a top speed of twenty-five knots.

Converted from a seaplane carrier, the redesign of the *Hōshō* was based in part on the reports of Japanese personnel who observed the operations of the HMS *Furious*. Funnels were relocated to starboard, and the superstructure was

removed entirely in the spring of 1919 and then replaced with a small starboard island that allowed an unobstructed 552-foot flight deck that sloped downward toward the forward edge to assist with takeoffs. During later modifications, the flight deck was leveled off. The designers incorporated a system of lights and mirrors along the flight deck to provide a solid sight picture for landing pilots. A total of six 5.5- and 3.1-inch antiaircraft guns were installed.

Two small hangars were completed on the same deck and accommodated a total of fifteen aircraft. Separate elevators serviced each hangar. Early aircraft types included the biplane Mitsubishi Type 10 fighter and B1M3 torpedo bomber, Nakajima A1N1 and A2N fighters, and the Yokosuka B3Y bomber. Aircraft types were steadily improved during the

The 14,700-ton USS *Wasp* was the last US Navy aircraft carrier laid down under the terms of the Washington Naval Treaty. The *Wasp* was constructed at the Fore River Shipyard in Quincy, Massachusetts, and commissioned on April 25, 1940. The design left some shortcomings in performance and, according to some observers, repeated mistakes that were made in the construction of an earlier light carrier, the USS *Ranger*. *National Naval Aviation Museum/2003.001.175*

1930s. During World War II, the flight deck was enlarged to accommodate advanced carrier aircraft, but the result rendered the carrier unsuitable for operations in the open sea.

The *Hōshō* served a purpose similar to that of the American *Langley*, being a platform for the refinement of carrier air operations and the development of naval air doctrine. In 1932, the carrier launched air raids against Chinese positions around the city of Shanghai, and with the outbreak of the Second Sino-Japanese War in 1937, the *Hōshō* was again deployed.

Like their future adversaries the USS *Lexington* and *Saratoga*, the first fleet carriers of the Imperial Japanese Navy were originally intended as battlecruisers. Conversion of the *Akagi* to an aircraft carrier began on November 19, 1923, at the Kure Naval Arsenal, and the carrier was launched on April 22, 1925, and commissioned on March 25, 1927. Upon completion, the *Akagi* displaced 27,300 tons and measured 857 feet long. Originally she was completed with three flight decks, the longest at 624 feet. Three hangars allowed the carrier to transport up to sixty aircraft. No island was constructed.

From 1935 to 1938, the *Akagi* underwent a significant course of rebuilding. An island was installed on the port side, and two flight decks were eliminated with the remaining flight deck extending nearly 819 feet. The hangar decks were enclosed, a third elevator was included, and aircraft capacity increased to more than eighty. The *Akagi* was powered by nineteen Kampon boilers that provided steam for four Gihon steam turbines generating 131,000 shaft horsepower and a top speed of thirty-two and one-half knots.

Prior to the outbreak of World War II, the *Akagi* played a significant role in the development of Japanese carrier doctrine, particularly the formation of carrier strike groups that concentrated carriers and their aircraft into a formidable force capable of projecting offensive air power thousands of miles from the Japanese home islands. The veracity inherent in such a doctrine was demonstrated with the attack on Pearl Harbor on December 7, 1941.

The *Kaga*, the second Japanese fleet carrier, was launched on November 7, 1921, at the Kawasaki Heavy Industries shipyard in the city of Kobe. Although conversion to an aircraft carrier was authorized in 1923, work was delayed for two years. The *Kaga* was commissioned on November 20,

continued on page 58

Above: Commissioned on December 27, 1922, seven months before the British *Hermes*, the Imperial Japanese Navy's *Hōshō* was the world's first warship designed and built as an aircraft carrier from the keel up. The *Hōshō* was quite diminutive in comparison to other carriers, displacing only 7,400 tons, and underwent a series of modifications during its career. Some of these were based on the observations of Japanese sailors who had witnessed operations aboard the British carrier HMS *Furious*. *Public domain*

Left: The Nakajima A1N fighter plane was a license-built copy of the British Gloster Gambet. The A1N entered service with the Imperial Japanese Navy in 1930, and about 150 were produced in Japan through 1932. The aircraft was armed with two 7.7-millimeter machine guns and capable of a top speed of 150 miles per hour. Obsolete by the mid-1930s, it was replaced by the Nakajima A2N, known in the Imperial Navy as the Type 90 carrier-based fighter. *Public domain*

The Japanese fleet carrier *Akagi* remains under construction at the Kure Naval Arsenal after its launching in 1925. The first fleet carrier of the Imperial Japanese Navy, the *Akagi* was converted from an original design as a battlecruiser, sharing this commonality with its future adversaries *Lexington* and *Saratoga* of the US Navy. Originally capable of carrying up to sixty planes, the *Akagi* displaced 27,300 tons and was built without an island, which was added later. *Kure Maritime History and Science Museum collection/Public domain*

AVIATION IRONY

Mitsubishi, one of the great Japanese aircraft manufacturers of the twentieth century, developed the Type 10 fighter, the first purpose-built carrier fighter plane in history, with the help of British aircraft designer Herbert Smith. During World War I, Smith designed the famed Sopwith Camel, Pup, Snipe, and Triplane. In 1921, Mitsubishi executives invited Smith and seven other British engineers to the city of Nagoya, Japan, to assist in establishing the company's aircraft division.

Smith's 1MF fighter bears a striking resemblance to earlier Sopwith models. It was designated the Type 10, replaced the British-made Gloster Sparrowhawk, and served with the Imperial Navy until 1930, when the Nakajima A1N fighter supplanted it. British pilot William Jordan, an associate of Smith, accomplished the first successful carrier takeoff and landing aboard a Japanese carrier, the *Hōshō*, on February 28, 1923.

Chauncey Milton Vought, an American aviation enthusiast better known as "Chance," also pioneered the development of carrier aircraft. Vought worked for the Wright Brothers and for Glenn Curtiss. His first design, the Mayo-Vought Simplex, was used by the British as a trainer in World War I. The Vought VE-7, equipped with an arresting hook, became the frontline fighter of the US Navy in the early 1920s and was the first aircraft to operate from the deck of the newly commissioned aircraft carrier USS *Langley* on October 17, 1922. A two-seat Vought UO-1 observation plane was the first US Navy aircraft launched by carrier catapult. Chance Vought died of septicemia on July 25, 1930, at the age of forty. However, his company continued to prosper and produce outstanding aircraft.

Vought VE-7 aircraft in various stages of completion sit on the floor of a manufacturing facility in 1923. The VE-7 was originally designed as a two-seat training aircraft for the US Army, and the US Navy later ordered the Vought plane as its first fighter. The VE-7 was among the complement of aircraft transported aboard the USS *Langley*, the navy's first aircraft carrier. *National Naval Aviation Museum/1996.253.7214.002*

Above: The island constructed aboard the *Akagi* during modifications conducted from 1935 to 1938 is clearly visible in this photo of the Imperial Japanese Navy aircraft carrier taken in April 1941, seven months prior to the attack on the US Pacific Fleet at Pearl Harbor. Note the protective padding around the exterior of the island, the sleek monoplanes on the flight deck, and the two aircraft carriers sailing off the port quarter of the *Akagi*. *Public domain*

Opposite above: The massive flight deck supports and downward stretching funnel of the Imperial Japanese Navy's fleet aircraft carrier *Kaga* are clearly seen in this photo as the warship lies at anchor in 1928. The *Kaga* was built by the Kawasaki Heavy Industries shipyard in Kobe and commissioned on November 20, 1929. Originally constructed with three flight decks, the *Kaga* underwent significant modifications in the mid-1930s, and two of the flight decks were removed in 1934–1935. *Public domain*

Opposite below: The flight deck of the Japanese aircraft carrier *Kaga* is crowded with biplanes as crewmen move about starting engines in this image taken in 1937. Although the *Kaga* had an identical displacement at 27,300 tons, it was slower than the Imperial Navy's first fleet carrier, the *Akagi*, with a top speed of just over twenty-seven knots. The *Kaga's* aircraft capacity was increased to eighty planes after modifications to its design in the 1930s. *Kure Maritime History and Science Museum collection/Public domain*

continued from page 54

1929, with a length of nearly 783 feet and a displacement of 27,300 tons. Like the *Akagi*, the *Kaga* was originally built with three flight decks and three hangars and had a capacity of sixty aircraft. The *Kaga* was slower than the *Akagi* with a top speed of twenty-seven and one-half knots powered by twelve Kampon boilers and four Kawasaki Brown-Curtis turbines generating ninety-one thousand shaft horsepower.

In June 1934, a yearlong reconstruction program eliminated two of the flight decks, allowing an increase of hangar space and boosting aircraft capacity to ninety. The remaining flight deck was extended to just over 815 feet. An early French transverse arresting gear design was replaced with a Japanese system, and a small island was raised to starboard. Problems with the funnels and exhaust were also addressed.

Commissioned on May 9, 1933, the Japanese light carrier *Ryūjō* was ostensibly built in compliance with the Washington Naval Treaty, which did not restrict the construction of carriers under ten thousand tons. Although the *Ryūjō* was officially

The Imperial Japanese Navy fleet aircraft carrier *Shōkaku* is shown at anchor in 1941. The *Shōkaku* was the first aircraft carrier constructed in Japan after the nation abrogated the Washington Naval Treaty in 1937. Displacing slightly more than twenty-six thousand tons, the *Shōkaku* was laid down in December of that year and commissioned on August 8, 1941. A second *Shōkaku*-class carrier, the *Zuikaku*, was laid down at the Kawasaki Kobe Yard on May 25, 1938, and launched six weeks after the *Shōkaku*. *Public domain*

The 17,300-ton *Hiryū* of the Imperial Japanese Navy is sometimes considered a warship of the *Sōryū* class. However, the *Hiryū* included many distinctive features that made it unique among light carriers. Similar to the larger *Akagi*, its island was constructed on the port side. The *Hiryū* was built at the Yokosuka Naval Arsenal and commissioned on July 5, 1939. This photograph was taken shortly after those ceremonies were concluded. *Kure Maritime History and Science Museum collection/Public domain*

a 7,100-ton warship, she actually displaced 10,600 tons. Despite its robust aircraft capacity of forty-eight planes, the light carrier experienced instability issues similar to those of the USS *Ranger* and underwent extensive modification twice during the 1930s.

Japanese aircraft carrier designers worked to correct the flaws in the *Ryūjō*'s construction and came up with a workable solution in the 15,900-ton *Sōryū*, laid down in November 1934 at the Kure Naval Arsenal, launched on December 21, 1935, and commissioned two years later. The *Sōryū* was designed as a carrier from inception and was just over 746 feet long with a flight deck of nearly 712 feet that was built over the ship's hull rather than integral to it and was supported by steel pillars at both ends.

An island was built on the starboard side, while upper and lower hangars were constructed and serviced by three elevators. In a tradeoff for speed, armor protection was minimal. Eight Kampon boilers produced steam for four geared turbines producing 152,000 shaft horsepower and a top speed of thirty-four knots. At the time of her completion, the *Sōryū* may well have been the fastest aircraft carrier in the world. Capable of carrying seventy-two aircraft, she was active during the Second Sino-Japanese War.

Although the 17,300-ton *Hiryū* is generally considered a *Sōryū*-class carrier, she was quite distinctive in her own right. Laid down at the Yokosuka Naval Arsenal on July 8, 1936, the *Hiryū* was launched on November 16, 1937, and commissioned on July 5, 1939. Her hull was broader than the *Sōryū*, and like the *Akagi* her island was placed on the port side in a failed experiment to facilitate air operations with carriers whose

islands were on the starboard side. Air traffic patterns, it was initially believed, would not impede one another. The remainder of the *Hiryū*'s design was virtually identical to that of the *Sōryū*.

In 1937, Japan abrogated the Washington Naval Treaty and other agreements, and the Imperial Navy soon began the construction of two new fleet carriers, each slightly larger than twenty-six thousand tons. The *Shōkaku* was constructed at the Yokosuka Naval Arsenal, laid down in December 1937, launched on June 1, 1939, and commissioned on August 8, 1941. The second *Shōkaku*-class carrier, *Zuikaku* was built at the Kawasaki Kobe Yard, laid down on May 25, 1938, launched on November 27, 1939, and commissioned on September 25, 1941, just weeks before the attack on Pearl Harbor.

The *Shōkaku*-class carriers were nearly 845 feet long with flight decks that extended beyond the superstructure and were characteristically supported by pillars. Their aircraft complements totaled nearly ninety planes, and as the Pearl Harbor operation neared, these included the vaunted Mitsubishi A6M Zero fighter, the Aichi D3A1 "Val" dive-bomber, and the versatile Nakajima B5N "Kate," both a horizontal and torpedo bomber.

During the two decades between the world wars, the aircraft carrier had been developed, refined, and positioned for an active role in naval warfare. Soon enough, the theory, conjecture, training, and speculation surrounding the carrier would be put to the ultimate test. During World War II, the aircraft carrier rapidly eclipsed the battleship as the weapon of decision on the high seas. A new era in naval warfare emerged with a thunderous roar.

FLATTOPS AT WAR

"Flight decks vibrated with the roar of aircraft engines warming up. Now a green lamp was waved in a circle. 'Take off!' The engine of our foremost fighter plane built up to a crescendo—and then the plane was off, safely. There were loud cheers as each plane rose into the air."

So wrote Lt. Cmdr. Mitsuo Fuchida of the Imperial Japanese Navy, remembering the moment that the first carrier-based aircraft of the attack on the American Pacific Fleet anchorage at Pearl Harbor got underway. The die was cast. There was no turning back. The aircraft carrier was the conduit for World War II to explode across the expanse of the Pacific Ocean and the Asian continent.

The sky was still dark as the well-trained Japanese pilots lifted off the decks of six aircraft carriers—*Akagi*, *Kaga*, *Sōryū*, *Hiryu*, *Shōkaku*, and *Zuikaku*—and set a

Crewmen of the USS *Enterprise* give the signal to fighter pilots to begin takeoff procedures in their Grumman F4F Wildcats. The Wildcat could not match the Japanese Zero fighter in every aspect of performance, but it served as the mainstay of the US Navy during the early months of World War II in the Pacific. Note the small bomb affixed under the wing of this Wildcat. *National Archives*

Crewmen aboard one of the six aircraft carriers of the Imperial Japanese Navy that launched hundreds of aircraft in a surprise attack against the US Pacific Fleet naval base at Pearl Harbor, Hawaii, on December 7, 1941, wave their caps as the planes take off toward their unsuspecting targets. *National Archives*

course for Pearl Harbor, some of them using the pleasant musical broadcast of a Honolulu radio station as a homing beacon to their intended targets. The planes were aloft following an often rehearsed choreography of prelaunch activities that had begun several hours earlier. Mechanics, armorers, handlers, and other support personnel had readied the planes for the attack. Pilots had been briefed. They drank a ceremonial toast of sake, the traditional Japanese rice wine, and waited. The order came; they climbed aboard their planes and then took off on a mission that had uncertain prospects for success but was sure to render dramatic consequences.

Although the Japanese had conceived of the aircraft carrier battle group and its concentrated aerial striking power, the Kidō Butai had not yet proven itself in battle. Prior operations had been limited to air strikes in China and training for the upcoming Pearl Harbor attack. On this day, extending the offensive capability of the Imperial Navy across thousands of miles, the doctrine of the carrier battle group would be proven in its ultimate context.

A sleepy Pearl Harbor was just stirring on Sunday, December 7, 1941, as the first Japanese planes appeared at approximately 7:55 a.m. above a mountain range to the north. American soldiers and sailors were astonished to see combat

aircraft with the red disc of the Rising Sun emblazoned on their wings and fuselages sweeping in to launch torpedoes against Battleship Row, diving to drop bombs on stationary targets, or remaining high aloft to release ordnance that crippled vessels, destroyed installations, and wreaked general havoc. Japanese fighters roared overhead, stitching ship and shore with machine gun fire.

Amid the confusion, an alert was flashed across the island of Oahu: "AIR RAID PEARL HARBOR—THIS IS NO DRILL!"

Years later, Fuchida wrote of his observations that fateful day. "Suddenly, a colossal explosion occurred in Battleship Row. A huge column of dark-red smoke rose to 1,000 feet, and a stiff shock wave reached our plane. A powder magazine must

Above: In this still frame from a Japanese propaganda newsreel, a Nakajima B5N "Kate" torpedo bomber, its lethal payload suspended in a sling beneath its fuselage, roars across the deck of a Japanese aircraft carrier en route to Pearl Harbor. The versatile Kate performed both torpedo and level bombing missions with the Imperial Navy's First Air Fleet early in World War II. *National Archives*

Following pages: Japanese dive-bombers, torpedo bombers, and fighters swarm in the skies above Pearl Harbor during the surprise attack on the US Pacific Fleet's naval base on December 7, 1941. The Japanese attacked in two waves, also hitting other US Navy, Marine Corps, and Army installations on the Hawaiian island of Oahu. This photo was taken from the submarine base at Pearl Harbor. The submarine shown in the foreground, the USS *Narwhal*, escaped undamaged. *National Archives*

This well-known aerial photo taken during the opening moments of the Japanese attack on Pearl Harbor depicts a Japanese torpedo plane banking away from Battleship Row adjacent to Ford Island as a geyser erupts from a torpedo strike on the battleship USS *West Virginia*. The original Japanese caption lauds the attack by the Imperial Navy's "Sea Eagles." *National Archives*

have exploded. The attack was in full swing; smoke from fires and explosions filled most of the sky over Pearl Harbor.

"Studying Battleship Row through binoculars, I saw the big explosion had been on the *Arizona*. She was still flaming fiercely, and since her smoke covered the *Nevada*, the target of my group, I looked for some other ship to attack. The *Tennessee* was already on fire, but next to her was the *Maryland*. I gave an order changing our target to this ship."

For two hours, the Japanese raiders sowed death and destruction on Pearl Harbor. Then they were gone, retreating rapidly to their floating airfields, the carriers. They had achieved complete surprise, and the situation across Oahu was chaotic.

Admiral Chūichi Nagumo, commander of the Japanese fleet, weighed his options. A third attack wave might finish off the Americans, inflicting so much damage that there would be no time to mount a serious challenge to the planned Japanese onslaught that included US and British territories and interests across the Pacific. But where were the American aircraft carriers?

The Japanese had launched their attack against Pearl Harbor well aware that the US Navy's carriers were not there. Could they be in a position to mount a counterstrike against Nagumo's own force? The safety of his own precious carriers was now paramount. The risk of an attack from American carrier-based planes was too great, and Nagumo chose to retire to the northwest at flank speed. In addition to being criticized by contemporary Imperial Japanese Navy officers, he has been criticized by various naval historians for the decision ever since. Regardless of whether it was the smart play, it was the safe play.

MITSUO FUCHIDA

Lieutenant Commander Mitsuo Fuchida led the Japanese attack on Pearl Harbor on December 7, 1941. He subsequently suffered an attack of appendicitis and barely escaped the sinking of the *Akagi* during the Battle of Midway. Fuchida survived the war and became a Christian missionary, dedicating the remainder of his life to missionary work and authoring the book *From Pearl Harbor to Golgotha*. He died in 1976 from complications of diabetes. *Zenith Press collection*

Admiral Isoroku Yamamoto, commander-in-chief of the Imperial Japanese Navy's Combined Fleet, warned against going to war with the United States. However, when conflict became inevitable he initiated the planning for the attack on Pearl Harbor, which demonstrated the destructive capability of the aircraft carrier battle group. Yamamoto died when his aircraft was shot down by American fighter planes above the island of Bougainville in the Solomons on April 18, 1943. *National Archives*

In the wake of the Pearl Harbor disaster, Adm. Chester W. Nimitz, a Texan and 1905 graduate of the US Naval Academy at Annapolis, assumed command of the shattered Pacific Fleet. Nimitz took calculated risks during defensive operations early in the conflict and then employed a powerful force of aircraft carriers and other warships that won the eventual victory over Japan during World War II in the Pacific. He died in 1966 at the age of eighty. *US Navy photo*

Admiral Jisaburō Ozawa directed successful Japanese aircraft carrier operations in the Indian Ocean early in World War II. In November 1942, he succeeded Chūichi Nagumo as commander of the Imperial Japanese Navy's primary aircraft carrier forces in the Pacific. Ozawa has been recognized as a skillful commander; however, he was defeated later in the war at the Battle of the Philippine Sea and also lost heavily during the Battle of Leyte Gulf. Ozawa died in 1966 at the age of eighty. *National Archives*

Crewmen aboard the USS *Enterprise* go about their routine amid aircraft parked on the warship's flight deck, some with their wings folded to save precious space. Douglas SBD Dauntless dive-bombers, the primary carrier-based bombing attack aircraft of the US Navy early in World War II, are prominent in this photograph. *National Archives*

Nagumo's conclusion was only the first of many significant decisions made by aircraft carrier task group commanders, both American and Japanese, across the vastness of the Pacific War during a four-year conflict that pitted carrier against carrier—a conflict the likes of which has never been seen since.

During the weeks that followed the Pearl Harbor attack, the Imperial Japanese Navy reigned supreme on the sea and in the skies above the Pacific Ocean. On land, the Japanese conquered tremendous amounts of territory, including Wake Island, Guam, Hong Kong, Singapore, and the entire Malay Peninsula. At sea, Nagumo's carriers struck with impunity, and Japanese planes pummeled the ships and facilities in the harbor at Darwin, Australia, on February 19, 1942. On March 26, Nagumo, with five of the six carriers that had devastated Pearl Harbor, sailed into the Indian Ocean. His dive-bombers sank the British cruisers HMS *Cornwall* and HMS *Dorsetshire* on April 5 in an action that came to be known as the Easter

Sunday Raid, and a detached force under Adm. Jisaburō Ozawa that included the carrier *Ryūjō* and six cruisers sank twenty-three British merchant ships in the Bay of Bengal in just a few days.

The day after the sinking of the two British cruisers, eighty-five Japanese Aichi D3A Val dive-bombers escorted by nine Mitsubishi A6M Zero fighters flew from Nagumo's carrier decks and caught the British carrier *Hermes* and its escorting destroyer HMS *Vampire* en route to the harbor at Trincomalee on the island of Ceylon (present-day Sri Lanka). More than two decades of service with the Royal Navy ended abruptly for the *Hermes*, pounded by no fewer than forty Japanese 250-pound bombs. The Japanese showered the *Vampire* as well. Both ships sank quickly, and 307 sailors from the *Hermes* lost their lives.

Adding insult to injury for the British, the Japanese submarine *I-6* spotted the *Saratoga* en route to a rendezvous

The USS *Langley*, the US Navy's first aircraft carrier, which was converted to a seaplane tender in the 1930s, lists heavily before sinking on February 27, 1942. Japanese Aichi D3A "Val" dive-bombers hit the *Langley* with five bombs off the coast of Java. *National Naval Aviation Museum/1998.409.076*

with the *Enterprise* 420 nautical miles southwest of Pearl Harbor on January 11, 1942, and put the carrier out of action for four months with a single torpedo hit. While the *Saratoga* was laid up at the Bremerton Navy Yard in Washington, she was modernized with improved radar, antiaircraft guns, and an anti-torpedo blister for the hull.

Meanwhile, the US Navy's other aircraft carriers in the Pacific did make their presence known to the Japanese. On February 1, 1942, aircraft from separate task forces centered on the USS *Yorktown* and USS *Enterprise* raided Japanese installations in the Gilbert and Marshall Islands. Although these were but pinpricks in the wake of the Japanese success at Pearl Harbor, the strikes did raise morale and helped American pilots and support personnel to gain practical experience in real wartime operations. The raids also raised concerns among senior Japanese military commanders regarding the security of their island defensive perimeter, influencing their subsequent offensive strategy. At the end of the month, the old carrier

continued on page 76

Lieutenant Colonel Jimmy Doolittle (left) and Capt. Marc A. Mitscher (right) pose on the flight deck of the USS *Hornet* during preparations for the April 18, 1942, bombing raid on Tokyo. Doolittle had received a decoration from the Japanese government during the interwar years, and as the bombs were loaded aboard his B-25 Mitchell medium bomber, he tacked the medal to one of them, effectively returning it to the sender. *US Air Force photo*

Right: On April 18, 1942, less than four months after the devastating Japanese attack on Pearl Harbor, the US military struck back at the homeland of Japan as North American B-25 Mitchell medium bombers of the Army Air Corps lifted off from the deck of the USS *Hornet* to bomb Tokyo. In this image, one of the B-25s labors into the air after the navy task force was spotted by a Japanese vessel and the decision was made to launch despite the increased risk. *US Navy photo*

Below: A North American B-25 Mitchell medium bomber takes off from the deck of the USS *Hornet*. The army pilots and crews of the B-25s trained for months in preparation for launching the traditionally land-based aircraft from the deck of a carrier. The raid inflicted little physical damage on its targets in and around the city of Tokyo; however, the Japanese perception that their home islands were safe from enemy attack was shattered. *US Air Force photo*

Left: The colorful cover of the book *Thirty Seconds Over Tokyo* by Capt. Ted W. Lawson alludes to the heroic air raid led by Lt. Col. Jimmy Doolittle to bomb the Japanese capital on April 18, 1942. The raid stunned the Japanese high command and prompted a series of fateful decisions as to its future conduct of the war in the Pacific. *Zenith Press collection*

Below: Hollywood actor Spencer Tracy starred as Lt. Col. Jimmy Doolittle in the feature film *Thirty Seconds Over Tokyo*, which dramatized the historic raid on the Japanese capital by sixteen North American B-25 Mitchell medium bombers flying from the USS *Hornet*. At the distance from which the bombers were launched, there was no opportunity for a return flight, and most of the raiders crash-landed their planes in China. *Zenith Press collection*

THIRTY SECONDS OVER TOKYO

By CAPT. TED W. LAWSON

15 cents

M-G-M presents the great motion picture

THIRTY SECONDS OVER TOKYO

A MERVYN LeROY PRODUCTION

with

VAN JOHNSON ★ ROBERT WALKER

PHYLLIS THAXTER • TIM MURDOCK • SCOTT McKAY
GORDON McDONALD • DON DeFORE • ROBERT MITCHUM
JOHN R. REILLY • HORACE McNALLY

and

SPENCER TRACY

as LIEUTENANT COLONEL JAMES H. DOOLITTLE

Screen Play by Dalton Trumbo   Based on the Book and Collier's Story by Captain Ted W. Lawson and Robert Considine
A METRO-GOLDWYN-MAYER PICTURE   Directed by MERVYN LeROY • Produced by SAM ZIMBALIST

continued from page 73

Langley, converted to a seaplane tender in the mid-1930s, fell victim to Japanese dive-bombers near the harbor of Tjilatjap (today's Cilacap) on the island of Java.

Even as they basked in the glory of their triumphs, Japanese senior commanders were unnerved by a tremendous example of American interservice cooperation. The plan required the approval of President Franklin D. Roosevelt himself. It was risky, but the American people were desperate for good news from the embattled Pacific. Sixteen North American B-25 Mitchell medium bombers of the US Army Air Forces flew from the deck of the carrier USS *Hornet* on April 18, 1942, and dropped bombs on the Japanese capital of Tokyo.

The impetus for the raid was Roosevelt's desire to win a propaganda victory against Japan, and it appeared that such a raid was feasible after US Navy captain Francis Low, a submarine officer, suggested that medium bombers might be capable of taking off from the short flight deck of a carrier. Lieutenant Colonel James Doolittle was selected to plan and lead the raid along with fifteen other crews of the 17th Bomb Group (Medium). Their B-25s were deemed most likely to succeed in the daring mission due to their range and bomb-load capacity. The USS *Hornet* was chosen to transport the Doolittle Raiders into hostile waters. When the last of the sixteen B-25s was lashed to the carrier's deck at Naval Air Station Alameda in San Francisco Bay, its tail section protruded beyond the stern of the carrier. The *Hornet*'s own air group was stowed on the hangar deck.

The *Hornet* set sail on April 2, 1942, and eleven days later joined with the *Enterprise* and numerous escorts near Midway Atoll in the Central Pacific. Plans to proceed to within four hundred nautical miles of the Japanese mainland went awry on the morning of April 18, when the task force was spotted by the Japanese patrol vessel *Nittō Maru*. The light cruiser USS *Nashville* promptly sank the enemy ship, but it was feared that it had gotten off a radio warning, compromising the security of the American force.

Rather than scrub the operation, Doolittle and Capt. Marc Mitscher, the *Hornet*'s commander, decided to take the gamble of launching immediately, even though the distance to Tokyo was well over six hundred nautical miles. To complicate matters, the seas were rough.

Doolittle piloted the first B-25 to launch, and he had only 467 feet of flight deck to work with. He gunned the twin engines and rolled forward, dipped toward the water in a forty-knot wind, and then clawed for altitude. Doolittle circled the *Hornet* twice. The other B-25s lifted off, formed up, and headed for Tokyo. To a man, the aviators knew that the distance might be too great to reach the Asian mainland, where it was hoped the aircrews could link up with friendly Chinese civilian or military personnel and eventually make their way to safety. The alternative was to ditch in the open sea.

The American bombers flew low to avoid detection and arrived over Tokyo at approximately noon, ironically while a civil defense drill was in progress. Bombs were dropped on targets in Tokyo and nearby Yokohama, causing little real damage.

As for the Doolittle Raiders, three of the eighty airmen were killed during the raid, one five-man crew was interned after landing in Soviet Russia, eight were captured by the Japanese, and the remainder, Doolittle among them, eventually returned to the United States or friendly areas. Three of the eight prisoners were executed, and a fourth died in captivity. All sixteen of the B-25s were lost, one of them to the Soviets. Twelve others crashed in China, and three ditched in the sea.

Doolittle became a national hero and received the Medal of Honor for his heroism. He was promoted to general rank and went on to command major air forces in the European Theater. He died at the age of ninety-six in 1993. When reporters asked President Roosevelt where the American bombers that hit Tokyo had come from, he grinned broadly and replied that they had been launched from Shangri-La, the mythical location in the Himalaya Mountains that was familiar to readers of the novel *Lost Horizon* by James Hilton, which was popular at the time.

Coupled with the earlier carrier raids on the Marshalls and Gilberts, the Doolittle Raid led to grave concerns within the Japanese military as to the security of the home islands, prompting Adm. Isoroku Yamamoto, commander-in-chief of the Japanese Combined Fleet, to seek a decisive battle that would destroy American carrier power in the Pacific once and for all. An upcoming operation to seize Port Moresby at the southeastern tip of the island of New Guinea would proceed. Its success would strengthen the Japanese perimeter and threaten Australia, the major Allied base of operations in the South Pacific. Yamamoto also began the planning for a major offensive to seize Midway Atoll in the Central Pacific and annihilate the American carriers.

Less than two weeks after the Doolittle Raid, the Japanese launched Operation MO with the dual objectives of capturing Port Moresby from the sea and seizing the island of Tulagi in the Solomons chain to establish a seaplane base. The ensuing Battle of the Coral Sea, fought from May 4 to May 8, 1942, is historically significant for several reasons. The engagement was the first carrier-versus-carrier battle in history, and the surface ships of the opposing sides never came within sight of each other. Further, for the first time in World War II, a Japanese offensive was turned away.

During the Battle of the Coral Sea, the relative inexperience of both navies in prosecuting carrier warfare became readily apparent. The Japanese launched a complex three-pronged offensive with an invasion force headed for Port Moresby, an occupation force to take Tulagi, and a carrier strike force that included the carriers *Shōkaku* and *Zuikaku* to provide muscle that would neutralize any American

The scourge of the skies above the Pacific, the Japanese Mitsubishi A6M Zero carrier-based fighter was the best aircraft of its kind early in World War II. In this photo, crewmen aboard the Imperial Navy aircraft carrier *Zuikaku* rest in the shadows of Zeros parked on the flight deck. Note the canvas covers that shade cockpits from the hot tropical sun. *Kure Maritime History and Science Museum collection/Public domain*

interference with the movement. Vice Admiral Shigeyoshi Inoue of the Japanese Fourth Fleet was in overall command, and Vice Adm. Takeo Takagi led the carrier strike force.

Admiral Chester W. Nimitz, the US Navy's commander-in-chief Pacific, was aware of the Japanese offensive as early as mid-April courtesy of navy cryptanalysts who had deciphered portions of a Japanese naval code the Americans called JN-25. Nimitz realized that a response was necessary. Although the *Hornet* and *Enterprise* were returning to Pearl Harbor from the Doolittle Raid and would be unable to participate, Nimitz detailed the carriers *Lexington* and *Yorktown*, under the command of Rear Adm. Frank Jack Fletcher, to disrupt the

Japanese plan. His instructions to Fletcher were deliberately vague: simply stop the enemy.

On May 3, the Japanese took Tulagi without a fight and Fletcher tipped his hand with an air strike by *Yorktown* planes that did little damage to the enemy on the island but alerted Takagi that an American carrier was in fact operating relatively close by. However, his carriers had previously been ordered to deliver nine Zero fighters to the huge forward base at Rabaul on the island of New Britain, and Takagi squandered a chance to strike the *Yorktown*. The two days required for the ferry operation put *Shōkaku* and *Zuikaku* too far away to launch an attack.

Lieutenant Commander Robert E. Dixon, a 1927 graduate of the US Naval Academy, receives the Navy Cross for heroism aboard the USS *Bunker Hill* on January 18, 1944. During the Battle of the Coral Sea, Dixon commanded a squadron of dive-bombers from the USS *Lexington* that participated in the sinking of the Japanese light carrier *Shōhō*. His radio message—"Scratch one flattop!"—became instantly famous. Dixon attained the rank of rear admiral during his naval career and died in 1981 at the age of seventy-five. *National Archives*

Lieutenant Paul D. Stroop served as a staff officer aboard the carrier USS *Lexington* during the Battle of the Coral Sea and wrote a dramatic account of the fighting from his perspective. A naval aviator and 1926 graduate of the US Naval Academy, Stroop rose to the rank of vice admiral. He died in 1995 at the age of ninety. *National Archives*

For the better part of three days, the opposing forces groped around the Coral Sea, the Solomons, and southern New Guinea looking for one another—at one time only seventy miles of water separated them. Early on the morning of May 7, a Japanese search plane sighted two American ships and reported contact with an aircraft carrier and a cruiser. Takagi took the pilot at his word and sent a heavy raid against the American ships, which was actually Fletcher's fueling group consisting of the fleet oiler *Neosho* and its escorting destroyer USS *Sims*. Both were sunk.

Takagi believed he had scored a major victory; however, *Yorktown* and *Lexington* remained temporarily unscathed. Simultaneous with the Japanese raid, Fletcher received a report from a *Yorktown* search aircraft that two Japanese carriers and four heavy cruisers were steaming 175 miles to the northwest. He launched every available plane, believing the raid was aimed at the Japanese fleet carriers. The *Yorktown* pilot corrected his error and clarified the report as four enemy ships, two heavy cruisers, and two destroyers.

Fletcher's planes were already aloft, and by chance they stumbled across the Japanese warships covering the Port Moresby invasion force. The fattest target was the 11,262-ton light carrier *Shōhō*, originally a submarine tender launched on June 1, 1935, which had undergone a lengthy conversion begun in 1941 and completed in January of the following year. Within ten minutes, she was a blazing wreck.

Lieutenant Commander Paul D. Stroop aboard the *Lexington* remembered the action reports received on the carrier's bridge: "It was a very successful attack, except that we had overkill on the carrier. I think probably we put at least seven torpedoes in the carrier and many bombs, and it was sunk immediately. Looking back on this, it was too bad that the attack hadn't been better coordinated and some of the force spread around on other ships. But this being our first battle of that kind, everybody went after the big prize, and they sank this rather soft carrier very quickly."

Stanley Johnson, a correspondent for the *Chicago Tribune*, was standing within earshot of the radio equipment aboard the *Lexington*. He heard the familiar voice of Lt. Cmdr. Bob Dixon, leader of the carrier's dive-bombers, across the squawk box. "All the tension on the carrier exploded the moment we hear Comdr. Dixon's voice come in strong and clear: 'Scratch one flattop! Dixon to carrier: Scratch one flattop!'"

Dixon's enthusiastic report was picked up by more print and radio media across the United States and became one of the early rallying cries of World War II in the Pacific. He received the Navy Cross for valor, served on carriers throughout the war, and rose to the rank of rear admiral. He died in 1981 at age seventy-five.

The loss of the *Shōhō* in itself was minor, but Inoue had no taste for undue risk and did not want the Port Moresby invasion force with its five thousand combat troops to proceed further without air cover. He ordered it to retire, thinking that another attempt could be made later. He was wrong.

The tactical errors on both sides continued. Late on the afternoon of May 7, Takagi sent dive-bombers, torpedo planes, and fighters to find and attack the American carriers. The Japanese pilots came up empty, but alert Grumman F4F Wildcat fighter pilots flying combat air patrol shot down nine of them. As daylight faded, six Japanese planes were lost when they tried to land on the *Yorktown*, believing the carrier

was their own. Another eleven either ditched in the ocean or crashed trying to make night landings on the pitching decks of *Shōkaku* and *Zuikaku*.

The next day, Dixon was in the air again. This time he and a younger pilot spotted Takagi's big carriers. Dixon sent the more inexperienced pilot back to the *Lexington* and stayed with the Japanese ships. Soon, both the *Lexington* and *Yorktown* were turned into the wind, launching planes. Heavy rain squalls and cloud cover offered some concealment for the Japanese, but the American carriers sailed in bright sunshine. While the American planes roared skyward, the Japanese launched more than seventy aircraft of their own.

Forty-one planes from the *Yorktown* never caught sight of the *Zuikaku* and concentrated their effort on the *Shōkaku*, visible in the intermittent fog and rain. Two bombs slammed into the big Japanese carrier. A third bomb, this one from a *Lexington* dive-bomber pilot, put the *Shōkaku* out of action with heavy damage, unable to launch or recover planes. Half of the *Lexington*'s aircraft never did find a target in the overcast.

At 11:20 a.m., the roles were reversed. The American carriers came under heavy attack. Stroop noted the event in his logbook aboard the *Lexington* and then looked on with grudging admiration.

Heavily damaged and billowing smoke, the USS *Lexington* takes on water during the Battle of the Coral Sea. The first US Navy aircraft carrier lost during the Pacific War, the *Lexington* took two bomb hits, and two torpedoes struck her port side. A destroyer stands by the stricken carrier, and a small boat in the foreground has already picked up some survivors. *National Naval Aviation Museum/2001.205.068*

A catastrophic explosion triggered by sparks that ignited fumes from ruptured aviation fuel tanks dooms the USS *Lexington*, already heavily damaged by Japanese dive bombers and torpedo planes during the Battle of the Coral Sea. Although 216 crewmen were killed, a total of 2,735 were rescued before the carrier sank. The Battle of the Coral Sea was a strategic victory for the US Navy, forcing the Japanese invasion force headed to Port Moresby on the southern tip of New Guinea to retire. *National Archives*

Sailors jump into the sea or descend on nets as they abandon the USS *Lexington*, hit by Japanese bombs and torpedoes during the Battle of the Coral Sea. Internal explosions caused by sparks that set off fumes from leaking aviation fuel tanks rocked the carrier and thwarted damage control efforts. Eventually, the *Lexington* was sunk by torpedoes from the destroyer USS *Phelps* just before 9:00 p.m. on May 8, 1942. *Hulton Archive/Getty Images*

The Japanese aircraft carrier *Shōkaku* takes evasive action while under attack by American carrier-based aircraft during the Battle of the Coral Sea on May 8, 1942. The *Shōkaku* was heavily damaged by three bombs and put out of action for the remainder of the battle with more than two hundred of its crew killed or wounded. The carrier was again heavily damaged during the Battle of the Santa Cruz Islands in October of that year and was finally sunk by torpedoes from the submarine USS *Cavalla* during the Battle of the Philippine Sea on June 19, 1944. *National Naval Aviation Museum/Robert L. Lawson Photograph Collection/1996.488.037.012*

"I can remember standing on the bridge and watching the enemy dive-bombers come down," he recalled. "These were fixed-landing-gear dive-bombers, and you were convinced that the pilot in the plane had the bridge of your ship in his sight. The instant he released his bomb, you could see the bomb taking a different trajectory from the aircraft itself. . . . The torpedo planes came in about the same time—a fine, nicely coordinated attack—and launched their torpedoes at about a thousand yards. First you saw the plane coming in and drop his torpedo in the water and saw it splash. Then you could see the wake of the torpedo directed toward the ship. . . ."

The *Lexington* was wracked by two bombs and as many as four torpedoes, which started fires and tore the carrier's hull below the waterline. A single bomb struck the *Yorktown*, penetrated four decks, and exploded, killing sixty-six sailors. For a time, it appeared that damage control parties aboard the *Lexington* had the situation in hand, but two catastrophic internal explosions doomed the great carrier, which had served the US Navy since 1927. At last, the order was given to abandon ship. More than 2,700

sailors were aboard the *Lexington*, but only 216 lost their lives. After the evacuation, torpedoes from an American destroyer finally sank the venerable carrier. *Yorktown* limped home to Pearl Harbor.

Both sides had had enough. As they disengaged, the outcome of the Battle of the Coral Sea was evaluated. It appeared at first to be a Japanese victory, since the Americans had lost the *Lexington* and the *Yorktown* had been heavily damaged. Such was probably the case on the tactical level. However, from a strategic perspective the Japanese had been denied the prize of Port Moresby. The *Shōhō* was sunk, while the *Shōkaku* was out of action for two months, and the *Zuikaku* air group was so thoroughly shot up that it took over a month to replace its losses in planes. The highly skilled pilots who died were irreplaceable.

In far-off Tokyo, Isoroku Yamamoto continued to plot his offensive against Midway with the knowledge that neither of his Coral Sea fleet carriers could participate in the operation set for early June. At Pearl Harbor, Chester Nimitz was armed with information that the Japanese planned a big push

On May 15, 1942, a Douglas SBD Dauntless dive-bomber attempts to land on the deck of the USS *Enterprise*. Three weeks later, Dauntlesses from the *Enterprise* played a key role in the defeat of the Japanese during the Battle of Midway. *National Archives*

and that Midway was their target. US Navy cryptanalysts at Station Hypo, working in the basement of the old administrative building at Pearl, had done it again.

Nimitz formulated a defensive plan, but he needed the badly damaged *Yorktown* battle worthy again to stand a real chance of victory in the face of Yamamoto's continuing superiority in planes and carriers. The coming Battle of Midway, fought from June 4 to 7, 1942, was destined to be the turning point of World War II in the Pacific.

The *Yorktown* arrived at Pearl Harbor on May 27, and it was estimated that adequate repairs would take a month. Nimitz allotted seventy-two hours, and carpenters, electricians, and other dry dock workers swarmed the carrier. In a minor miracle, the *Yorktown* set sail on May 30 to a rendezvous with the *Enterprise* and *Hornet* northeast of Midway, 1,100 miles distant from Pearl Harbor and appropriately named Point Luck. Admiral Fletcher flew his flag in *Yorktown* with Task Force 17, while Adm. Raymond A. Spruance commanded the *Enterprise* and *Hornet* and their escorts, designated Task Force 16. If the three American carriers remained undetected long enough, they might ambush the Japanese and win a decisive victory against long odds.

Fletcher was senior and in overall command, but as the Battle of Midway unfolded Spruance operated with increasing autonomy. Formerly a cruiser commander, Spruance was not an aviator. He was taking the place of William F. "Bull" Halsey, the US Navy's most experienced carrier admiral, who was hospitalized with a serious skin infection.

Throughout World War II, the senior staff of the Imperial Japanese Navy favored complex battle plans, often dividing its forces. Yamamoto's Midway scheme was true to form. Initially, a feint would be made against the islands of Attu and Kiska in the Aleutians far to the north. An invasion force was to transport five hundred troops to capture Midway, and a carrier force under Admiral Nagumo that included four veterans of the Pearl Harbor attack—*Akagi*, *Kaga*, *Sōryū*, and *Hiryū*, carrying more than two hundred aircraft—was to provide air cover and annihilate any American carriers that challenged the operation. Yamamoto himself sailed aboard the super battleship *Yamato*, leading yet another overwhelming force of warships that would, if necessary, engage the Americans in a surface battle.

An American search plane spotted the Japanese invasion force on the morning of June 3, but air attacks launched from

continued on page 90

Heavily damaged during the Battle of the Coral Sea, the USS *Yorktown* lies in dry dock at Pearl Harbor in May 1942. The damage to the *Yorktown* was expected to take weeks to repair. However, Adm. Chester W. Nimitz, commander-in-chief of the Pacific Fleet, allotted only seventy-two hours because the carrier was badly needed during the Battle of Midway. *US Navy photo*

Right: Crewmen prepare a Douglas SBD Dauntless dive-bomber for takeoff on the flight deck of the USS *Yorktown* during the Battle of Midway, fought June 4–7, 1942. Dauntlesses from the *Yorktown* and her sister carrier the USS *Enterprise* struck the decisive blow of the Pacific War, destroying four Japanese aircraft carriers during the battle. *National Naval Aviation Museum/1996.488.253.620*

Below: The propeller of a Douglas SBD Dauntless dive bomber belonging to one of the scout bombing squadrons assigned to the USS *Enterprise* continues to turn after the plane has crashed on the carrier's deck during a landing attempt. Crewmen hustle to the assistance of the pilot and rear gunner. During the early months of World War II in the Pacific, carrier-based Dauntless formations were divided into scout and bombing squadrons. The Navy later abandoned this structure. *National Archives*

Above: In this photograph taken from a nearby plane, US Navy Douglas SBD Dauntless dive-bombers prepare to attack a Japanese aircraft carrier during the Battle of Midway. Within minutes, three Japanese carriers—*Akagi*, *Kaga*, and *Sōryū*—were reduced to flaming wrecks, and the course of World War II in the Pacific had been altered in favor of the United States. At least one Japanese carrier, visible in this image, is already burning. *National Archives*

Left: A disabled US Navy Douglas Dauntless dive-bomber ditches in the Pacific Ocean near the cruiser USS *Astoria* during the Battle of Midway. The Dauntless was a navy workhorse early in World War II but was later supplanted by other aircraft such as the Grumman TBF Avenger and the Curtiss SB2C Helldiver. *National Naval Aviation Museum/1996.253.588*

continued from page 87

Midway produced no positive results. The following morning, Nagumo's carriers nosed through fog and rain until the weather improved enough to launch more than one hundred planes to soften up Midway for the impending landings and neutralize its troublesome airstrip.

While the attackers were returning to the Japanese carriers, the strike commander radioed that a second raid against Midway was necessary. Nagumo was then on the horns of a dilemma. He had held some aircraft in reserve to strike the American aircraft carriers if they were sighted. These planes were armed with torpedoes; if he decided to attack Midway a second time, they would have to exchange the torpedoes for bombs to hit land targets. While the changeover was taking place, he could continue to land his planes returning from the first Midway raid along with most of his Zero fighters then flying combat air patrol—all of which were critically low on fuel.

The switch would cost Nagumo precious time, but the appearance of American land-based bombers, whose attacks again resulted in no damage to his force, helped him decide to rearm the reserve planes with bombs for a second Midway strike. Just as this effort was getting underway, Nagumo received a report from a search plane indicating that ten American ships were sailing about two hundred miles to the northeast, including an aircraft carrier.

Nagumo vacillated. He considered ordering those planes already rearmed with bombs to take off against Midway. Those still armed with torpedoes could attack the American carrier. At long last, he decided to arm all available planes with torpedoes and continue to recover the planes that remained aloft.

The aircraft maintenance crews aboard the four Japanese carriers knew that time was of the essence. They worked feverishly, stretching fuel lines across the decks and muscling bombs out of the way as they attached torpedoes to the Mitsubishi B5N Kates being readied against the sighted American carrier. The bombs lay in the open. They could be secured later. These frenetic operations left Nagumo's carriers highly vulnerable.

The Americans were busy, too. The Japanese carriers were sighted around 5:30 on the morning of June 4, and though their aircraft would be at the limit of their range, Fletcher and Spruance turned the *Yorktown*, *Enterprise*, and *Hornet* into the wind and launched virtually every attack aircraft they had:

In this stylized painting of the decisive action during the Battle of Midway by artist Wilfred Hardy, a Japanese aircraft carrier blazes as US Navy Douglas Dauntless dive-bombers pull out of their dives and begin to take evasive action against enemy fighters during the perilous flight back to their carrier. In the span of a few minutes, American dive-bombers devastated three Japanese aircraft carriers, the *Akagi*, *Kaga*, and *Sōryū*. A fourth, the *Hiryū*, was sunk in a later raid. *Wilf (Wilfred) Hardy/Private Collection/© Look and Learn/ Bridgeman Images*

Right: Admiral Chūichi Nagumo led the Japanese aircraft carrier battle group that devastated Pearl Harbor and other US military installations on Oahu. His carriers then embarked on a successful operation in the Indian Ocean. However, his string of successes came to an abrupt end with the loss of four aircraft carriers at the Battle of Midway. Nagumo committed suicide on the island of Saipan in the Marianas on July 6, 1944. *National Archives*

Below: A plume of smoke and water shoots skyward as an aerial torpedo strikes the port side of the USS *Yorktown*, and black splotches of antiaircraft fire burst overhead while the carrier reels under attack by planes from the Japanese carrier *Hiryū* during the Battle of Midway. Although the *Yorktown* was eventually lost, within hours of this attack the *Hiryū* would become the fourth Japanese carrier sunk by American dive-bombers during the battle. *National Archives*

Left: The cruiser USS *Astoria* stands by to assist in the evacuation of crewmen from the USS *Yorktown*, seriously damaged by Japanese bombs and torpedoes during the Battle of Midway. *US Navy photo*

Below: Sailors aboard the USS *Yorktown* walk along the heavily listing flight deck of the damaged warship during the Battle of Midway. Effective damage control offered a glimmer of hope that the carrier might be saved. However, torpedoes from the Japanese submarine *I-168* sank the *Yorktown* on June 7, 1942. The attending destroyer USS *Hammann* was also lost to torpedoes fired from the submarine. The submarine USS *Scamp* sank the *I-168* on July 27, 1943. *National Archives*

150 Douglas SBD Dauntless dive-bombers, Douglas TBD Devastator torpedo planes, and their escort of Wildcat fighters.

American naval air doctrine called for coordinated dive-bomber and torpedo attacks against enemy targets. However, some formations lost their way. Others arrived at the point in the expanse of the Pacific where the Japanese were supposed to be and found nothing but miles of blue ocean. There would be no coordinated attack. Eventually, those American planes that did find the Japanese carriers went in on their own initiative.

Ironically, the lack of coordination worked in the Americans' favor. The lumbering torpedo planes found the Japanese first, and the covering Zero fighters tore into them like wolves. The Devastators were shot down in great numbers, and not a single torpedo struck home.

As the situation appeared to be under control, Nagumo ordered his carriers to launch their aircraft. The covering Japanese fighters flew at low altitude chasing the last of the American torpedo bombers, and as the first aircraft roared

Actors Charlton Heston and Henry Fonda led an all-star cast in the feature film *Midway*, released in 1976. The film blends historical and fictionalized characters and events along with archival footage to produce a typically Hollywood version of the pivotal World War II battle. *Zenith Press collection*

Caught in a death dive, a Japanese aircraft bursts into flames as antiaircraft fire from the USS *Enterprise* and surrounding escorts strikes home. This action occurred during the Battle of the Eastern Solomons in August 1942, one in a series of naval engagements that contributed to the outcome of the fight for the island of Guadalcanal. During the battle three Japanese bombs struck the *Enterprise*, which underwent six weeks of repairs at Pearl Harbor. *National Naval Aviation Museum/Robert L. Lawson Photograph Collection/1996.488.272.009*

down the flight deck of a Japanese carrier, a lookout called out an ominous warning. Fifty American dive-bombers, unmolested by the Zeros, came screaming down on the pride of the Imperial Japanese Navy.

Lieutenant Commander John S. Thach, leading the Wildcat fighters of squadron VT-3 from the *Yorktown*, watched the sequence of events. "Then I saw this glint in the sun," he later wrote, "and it just looked like a beautiful silver waterfall, these dive-bombers coming down. I'd never seen such superb dive-bombing. It looked to me like almost every bomb hit."

In a matter of seconds, the fate of nations was decided. The character of the Pacific War changed. American bombs plowed through planes armed and fueled on flight decks and exploded among stacked ordnance and exposed fuel lines. Three of Nagumo's carriers—*Akagi*, *Kaga*, and *Sōryū*—blazed like funeral pyres. Each later sank.

Only the *Hiryū*, obscured in a rain squall, was untouched. Rapidly, the lone Japanese carrier launched eighteen bombers

and six fighters against the *Yorktown*. Most of the Japanese planes were shot down, but three bombs shook the tough carrier. A second Japanese raid put two torpedoes into the *Yorktown*. Damage control efforts stabilized the listing carrier, but on June 6 a Japanese submarine torpedoed both the *Yorktown* and the escorting destroyer *Hammann*. The *Hammann* went down within minutes, and the *Yorktown* sank the next day.

The stubborn *Hiryū*, however, did not last long. Twenty-four Dauntlesses, including ten orphans from the *Yorktown*, took off from the *Enterprise* on the afternoon of June 4 and hit the last Japanese carrier with four bombs. The *Hiryū* followed the other Japanese carriers to the bottom of the Pacific.

The Midway defeat was disastrous for the Japanese, who lost four carriers, a cruiser, 332 planes, and more than 2,000 men. The Americans lost the gallant *Yorktown*, the destroyer *Hammann*, 137 planes, and 307 killed in action. Among the most one-sided victories in naval history, the Battle of Midway put the Japanese on the defensive for the balance of World War II.

Yamamoto considered an attempt to draw the Americans into a surface engagement, but then canceled the Midway landings and withdrew. Admiral Spruance declined to pursue and ordered his carriers to set course for Pearl Harbor. He

Launched in the spring of 1931, the light carrier *Ryūjō* would become the principal Imperial Japanese Navy casualty during the Battle of the Eastern Solomons. At least three American bombs and possibly an aerial torpedo hit the carrier, which sank after darkness fell on August 24, 1942. More than 120 of the carrier's crew were killed or wounded during the action. As seen in the left photo, the chrysanthemum emblem of the Japanese royal house crowned the carrier's bow.
Kure Maritime History and Science Museum collection/Public domain

remembered that Nimitz had warned him to safeguard his carriers and apply the principle of "calculated risk." The risks he and Fletcher had taken made all the difference.

With the Midway victory, the US Navy wrested the initiative in the Pacific from the Japanese. On August 7, 1942, elements of the 1st Marine Division landed on the island of Guadalcanal in the Solomons, where it was known that the enemy had begun construction of an airstrip that could threaten Allied communication and supply lines from Australia throughout the South Pacific. The ensuing struggle for Guadalcanal lasted six months with lengthy periods of stalemate punctuated by horrific combat. The marines seized the Japanese airstrip, completed it, and named it Henderson Field in honor of a pilot killed in action at Midway. In December, they were relieved by the US Army's Americal Division. Guadalcanal was not secured until the Japanese withdrew their troops in February 1943.

Three US Navy task forces, each with a single carrier, initially supported the Guadalcanal landings. USS *Wasp* led Task Force 18, USS *Saratoga* Task Force 11, and USS *Enterprise* Task Force 16. Admiral Fletcher maintained tactical command. For the Americans, carrier air power coupled with the land-based planes of the "Cactus Air Force" flying from Henderson Field played a pivotal role at Guadalcanal as control of the skies and seas around the island were prerequisites to the eventual victory. Two major carrier battles occurred during the arduous campaign, and the US Navy paid dearly in its effort.

By mid-August both sides were occupied with augmenting their offensive capability on Guadalcanal, with the Japanese

reinforcing their troops on the island, the Americans sending planes to Henderson Field, and both opposing fleets anticipating a carrier battle. On August 21, Admiral Nagumo sailed from the Japanese base at Truk in the Caroline Islands with a strong force including the fleet carriers *Shōkaku* and *Zuikaku* along with the 10,150-ton light carrier *Ryūjō*. Heavy warships in two additional task groups also moved to the Solomons, while scores of land-based aircraft from Rabaul would support an effort to locate and attack the American carriers.

Fletcher's carriers had retired to positions of relative safety four hundred miles south of Guadalcanal, but the marines' victory at the Battle of the Tenaru River (actually the Ilu River) brought the naval force back toward the island with the dual mission of supporting the marines holding Henderson Field and engaging the growing Japanese naval presence.

On August 24, 1942, the opposing carrier forces fought the Battle of the Eastern Solomons. At about 9:30 a.m., Fletcher received a report that confirmed the presence of the *Ryūjō*. However, he was concerned that the Japanese had already pinpointed his own location and waited four hours to launch a strike against the Japanese carrier. Actually, the first sighting of the *Enterprise* and *Saratoga* was radioed to Nagumo shortly after 2:00 p.m. While the *Shōkaku* and *Zuikaku* launched aircraft to hit the American carriers, Fletcher was notified that the big Japanese flattops had been found. Nagumo doubled down and sent a second raid aloft at 4:00 p.m.

At about the same time, while aircraft from the *Ryūjō* attacked Henderson Field, the *Saratoga*'s dive-bombers and torpedo planes fell upon the light carrier and scored hits with

Above: The last of three Japanese bombs that struck the USS *Enterprise* during the Battle of the Eastern Solomons on August 24, 1942, explodes on the flight deck of the embattled warship. The *Enterprise* was heavily damaged; however, its disciplined damage control parties performed superbly, and the carrier resumed flight operations later in the day. The photographer who took this photograph was killed by the blast. *National Archives*

Opposite: Lieutenant David McCampbell, serving as the landing signal officer aboard the USS *Wasp*, signals a plane approaching the carrier's flight deck. McCampbell went on to become the highest scoring fighter ace of the US Navy during World War II with thirty-four confirmed aerial kills. Behind McCampbell is Ensign George E. "Doc" Savage, the assistant landing signal officer. This photo was probably taken in early 1942. *National Archives*

at least three bombs and one torpedo. Uncontrollable fires raged, and the *Ryūjō* sank later in the day. The pilots returning from the Henderson Field strike had no place to land and ditched in the sea.

A few minutes after *Ryūjō* was crippled, the planes of Nagumo's first raid were picked up by radar aboard the *Saratoga*. At about 4:30, the veteran Japanese dive-bomber and torpedo pilots split up for a simultaneous attack. The *Enterprise* was the nearest target and took the brunt of the assault. Within two minutes, the carrier took three Japanese bomb hits. The first struck the flight deck and penetrated three decks below the aft elevator before it exploded, killing or wounding more

than one hundred sailors. The second exploded only fifteen feet away from the first and started fires that set off a secondary explosion of five-inch ammunition. Another thirty-five sailors died. The third bomb hit the flight deck forward and detonated on impact, blowing a ten-foot-wide hole. Efficient damage control parties put out fires and stopped flooding, while the hole in the flight deck was patched. Amazingly, in about an hour the *Enterprise* resumed flight operations.

The second Japanese air raid failed to find the American carriers, while dive-bombers from the *Saratoga* could not locate the Japanese fleet carriers but stumbled across the seaplane tender *Chitose*, scoring a couple of near misses that

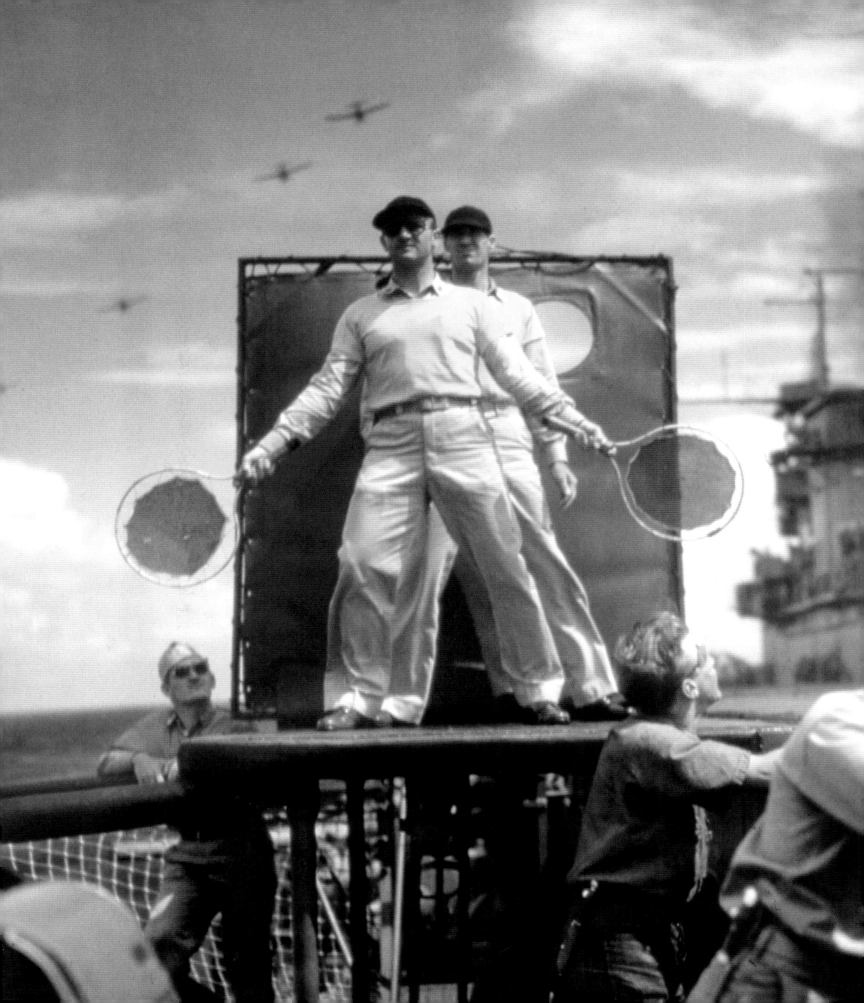

Pictured while steaming at sea, the USS *Wasp* reached the waters around the island of Guadalcanal in the Solomons in early August 1942. The carrier had steamed south to refuel later in the month and did not participate in the Battle of the Eastern Solomons. *National Archives*

caused significant damage. During the night both carrier forces retired. The following day planes from Henderson Field damaged a Japanese cruiser and sank a destroyer.

The Battle of the Eastern Solomons is generally considered an American victory for two reasons: the Japanese suffered greater damage to their naval contingent, and their reinforcements intended for Guadalcanal were delayed. However, the struggle for the island was by no means over.

During the early months of the war in the Pacific, the *Wasp* had operated with the US Atlantic Fleet and assisted the British Home Fleet ferrying fighter planes to the Mediterranean island of Malta. In June 1942, the carrier was transferred to the Pacific, and its aircraft supported the marine landings on Guadalcanal. The *Wasp* was refueling south of the combat zone and did not participate in the Battle of the Eastern Solomons.

The threat of attack from Japanese submarines was constant in the close waters surrounding Guadalcanal, and a week after the Battle of the Eastern Solomons the submarine *I-26* put a single torpedo into the starboard side of the *Saratoga* slightly

aft of the island. The carrier took on water and listed slightly, but more troublesome was the damage to the electrically generated propulsion system. The *Saratoga* was dead in the water for a short time, then taken under tow, and finally reached Pearl Harbor for extensive repairs.

On September 15, the *Wasp*, the *Hornet*, and the new battleship USS *North Carolina* led a convoy transporting the 7th Marine Regiment to reinforce Guadalcanal. The carrier completed the launch and recovery of combat air patrol planes, and moments after the last Wildcat fighter touched down a lookout yelled ominously, "Three torpedoes, three points forward of the starboard beam!"

The Japanese submarine *I-19* had fired a spread of six torpedoes—probably the most destructive of the Pacific War— and Capt. Forrest Sherman took evasive action, ordering the rudder hard to starboard. The effort was futile, and in rapid succession three struck home near the *Wasp*'s starboard magazines and tanks filled with aviation fuel. Two more torpedoes passed ahead of the carrier, and one of them hit the destroyer USS *O'Brien* on the port bow as the other hissed

Left: Grumman F4F Wildcat and Supermarine Spitfire fighter planes are parked on the flight deck of the USS *Wasp* in April 1942. After supporting the US occupation of Iceland in 1941, the carrier undertook joint operations with the British Royal Navy and ferried fighter aircraft to the embattled island of Malta in the Mediterranean Sea on two occasions. In June 1942, the *Wasp* was transferred to the Pacific. *National Naval Aviation Museum/1996.253.7386.029*

Below: Engulfed in flames following hits from three torpedoes fired by the Japanese submarine *I-19* off Guadalcanal, the USS *Wasp* burns furiously on the afternoon of September 15, 1942. Six torpedoes were fired in the spread, and five scored hits. The destroyer *O'Brien* and the battleship *North Carolina* were damaged. The *Wasp* sank at approximately 9:00 p.m. with 193 men killed and 366 wounded. *Library of Congress*

An American pilot secures himself in the cockpit of his plane on the flight deck of an aircraft carrier prior to takeoff. The confines of the plane's cockpit were jammed with gauges and other equipment, and pilots frequently found it difficult to extricate themselves in the event that it became necessary to bail out. *National Archives*

past to its stern. After a running time of about eight minutes, the last torpedo from *I-19* slammed into the port side of the *North Carolina*, ripping a hole thirty-two feet by eighteen feet and killing five sailors.

The *Wasp* slowed to ten knots as fires raged, setting off ammunition and torching planes on the hangar deck. The carrier shuddered with internal explosions, and the order to abandon ship was passed within the hour. At 9:00 p.m., approximately six hours after the carrier was hit, torpedoes from an American destroyer sent the blackened hulk to the bottom.

By October, the Japanese and American forces on Guadalcanal had slugged with one another for nearly three

months. Now, they were like a pair of punch-drunk boxers, neither side willing to concede. Both fed reinforcements into the fight. The Japanese also marshaled their naval power at the anchorage of Truk and then sortied to the waters off the Solomons with four carriers, five battleships, eight heavy cruisers, four light cruisers, and twenty-seven destroyers. Lethal Japanese submarines continued to prowl, and more than two hundred fighters and bombers were based at Rabaul. Their aim was to support a massive push to capture Henderson Field and inflict decisive damage on the American naval presence.

When the *Enterprise* returned to the combat zone from two months of repairs at Pearl Harbor, the US Navy could muster a countering force less than half the size of its enemy. Although the marines held onto Henderson Field, the naval force consisted only of the *Enterprise* and *Hornet*, the new battleships *Washington* and *South Dakota*, five heavy and two light cruisers, and twelve destroyers. The carrier forces were under the tactical command of Rear Adm. Thomas Kinkaid, while Adm. Willis Lee commanded a direct support task force closer to Guadalcanal.

Characteristically, the Japanese divided their strength into three separate forces under Adms. Nagumo, Nobutake Kondō, and Hiroaki Abe. Meanwhile, Nimitz lost confidence in his overall commander in the Solomons, Vice Adm. Robert L. Ghormley, and replaced him with the aggressive Halsey, who immediately went looking for a fight.

He found it.

Although their army's land offensive failed after five days of fighting on Guadalcanal, the Japanese admirals were undeterred. As the two carrier forces closed within two hundred miles of one another on the morning of October 26, reconnaissance aircraft from the *Enterprise* found Nagumo and the old nemesis carriers *Shōkaku* and *Zuikaku* accompanied by the light carrier *Zuihō*. Within fifteen minutes, a Japanese search plane located the *Hornet*. The two sides scrambled to get air attacks launched.

The Japanese were airborne first with twenty-one Val dive-bombers, twenty Kate torpedo bombers, and an escort of twenty-one Zero fighters. The *Hornet* and *Enterprise* launched seventy-three planes. A pair of scouting Dauntless dive-bombers went into action on the pilots' own initiative and hit the *Zuihō* with five-hundred-pound bombs, seriously damaging the Japanese carrier and halting further flight operations.

The opposing air strikes passed one another in flight, and each side lost some planes in dogfights. A few minutes later, the *Hornet*'s dive-bombers found the *Shōkaku* and scored multiple hits that started fires and demolished the Japanese carrier's flight deck. American planes also damaged a cruiser and a destroyer.

Just before 9:00 a.m., the Japanese aircraft attacked. The *Enterprise* was temporarily obscured by a rain squall, and the

Left: During the Battle of the Santa Cruz Islands in October 1942, crewmen aboard the USS *Enterprise* signal the course and speed of a Japanese aircraft carrier that has been sighted to pilots readying for takeoff while also informing them to proceed without attempting to rendezvous with aircraft from the carrier *Hornet*. The *Hornet* was hit by three bombs and three torpedoes during the battle, while a pair of Japanese pilots intentionally crashed their damaged planes into the carrier, which sank in the predawn hours of October 27, 1942. *National Naval Aviation Museum/1996.488.005.001*

Below: Puffs of black smoke from intense and accurate antiaircraft fire dot the sky as the USS *Enterprise* attempts to fend off attacking Japanese planes during the Battle of the Santa Cruz Islands. The carrier suffered extensive damage but underwent repairs at New Caledonia and played a key role in the decisive Naval Battle of Guadalcanal the following month. *National Archives*

Crewmen aboard the escort carrier USS *Santee* load ammunition for the rear-facing .30-caliber machine gun of a Douglas SBD Dauntless dive-bomber in October 1942. The *Santee* served on convoy escort duty in the Atlantic and provided air support for the Allied landings on the coast of North Africa during Operation Torch before transferring to the Pacific in February 1944. *National Archives*

Hornet absorbed the initial fury. Future Rear Adm. Francis D. Foley was serving as air operations officer aboard the *Hornet* during the engagement that came to be known as the Battle of the Santa Cruz Islands. He remembered the events of that fateful morning.

"Despite very effective antiaircraft fire, a heavy bomb hit the flight deck aft, causing severe damage and numerous casualties," Foley wrote. "Two near misses shook us up. The leader of a flight of dive bombers, his plane on fire, bore on in, hitting us with three bombs; one detonated on the flight deck abreast the island, another at the forward part of the stack, and the third was a dud which penetrated to the gallery deck. The

fuselage shattered the signal bridge, causing twelve casualties and a stubborn gasoline fire, all just over my head."

The fuselage to which Foley referred was that of the Japanese flight leader's plane. Realizing his aircraft was in flames, the pilot chose to crash into the *Hornet* rather than the water. Japanese torpedo planes put two lethal torpedoes in the *Hornet* on the starboard side amidships. The carrier lost all power, but three destroyers sprayed water on the fires, which were brought under control. Soon, more Japanese planes arrived, and these concentrated on the now visible *Enterprise*. Two bomb hits killed forty-four sailors and wounded another seventy-five.

The British Royal Navy aircraft carrier HMS *Glorious* steams ahead in this photo taken from the deck of the nearby carrier HMS *Ark Royal*. The image, from May 1940, turned out to be the last of the *Glorious*, which was sunk by gunfire from the German battlecruisers *Scharnhorst* and *Gneisenau* in early June. The destroyer sailing forward of the *Glorious* is the HMS *Diana*. *US Navy collection*

Later in the afternoon, another Japanese aerial torpedo hit the *Hornet*, causing a substantial list and knocking out power for a second time. Reluctantly, Halsey ordered American destroyers to sink the stricken carrier with torpedoes and gunfire, but to no avail. Japanese destroyers ultimately sent the abandoned carrier to the bottom.

Although the Battle of the Santa Cruz Islands may be considered a tactical Japanese victory, the effort to take Guadalcanal and eradicate the US naval presence in the vicinity had been thwarted. Once again, the Japanese counted the cost in experienced aircrews. Some returning pilots were so visibly shaken that they could not communicate.

The air officer aboard the carrier *Junyō* observed, "We searched the sky with apprehension. There were only a few planes in the air in comparison with the numbers launched several hours before. . . . The planes lurched and staggered onto the deck, every single fighter and bomber bullet holed. . . . As the pilots climbed wearily from their cramped cockpits, they told of unbelievable opposition, of skies choked with antiaircraft shell bursts and tracers."

After two weeks of repairs at New Caledonia, the damaged *Enterprise* returned to action and took part in the Naval Battle of Guadalcanal in November, primarily an engagement between surface ships and land-based aircraft that finally settled the issue at Guadalcanal in favor of the Americans. For a critical period, the *Enterprise* was the only operational American carrier in the entire Pacific. The Japanese carriers damaged in the Battle of the Santa Cruz Islands were out of action for months.

Following the Guadalcanal victory, American forces maintained the offensive in the Pacific on land and sea. The primary strike weapon of the US Navy from 1943 through the end of the war was on the way, and the *Essex*-class aircraft carrier ultimately became the stuff of legend.

When the United States entered World War II on December 7, 1941, Great Britain had been at war with Nazi Germany for more than two years. The aircraft carriers of the Royal Navy played key roles in the defense of the island nation, and by 1942 their tactical employment was being reshaped through combat experience.

The initial British carrier participation in World War II was inauspicious. On September 17, 1939, two weeks after Britain declared war on Germany, the HMS *Courageous* patrolled the Atlantic off the coast of Ireland. For two hours the German submarine *U-29* tracked the carrier. After dark, with two escorting destroyers released to assist a merchant ship under attack, the carrier turned into the wind to launch aircraft. In rapid succession, two torpedoes from the *U-29* hit the port side of the old carrier, which capsized and sank in twenty minutes, taking more than five hundred crewmen with it. With the loss of the *Courageous*, the Admiralty decided against putting carriers at further risk on antisubmarine patrols.

In April and May 1940, the *Glorious* and *Ark Royal* supported the ultimately failed British Army operations in Norway. By June, the *Glorious* was returning to the primary Home Fleet anchorage at Scapa Flow in the Orkney Islands in the north of Scotland. At the same time, the Kriegsmarine (German navy) battlecruisers *Scharnhorst* and *Gneisenau*, each with eleven-inch main guns, were prowling the waters off Norway for British merchant shipping to attack.

Around 4:00 p.m. on June 8, the Germans spotted the smoke from the *Glorious*'s stack, and within minutes the British were aware of the nearby presence of other warships. The destroyer *Ardent* was sent to reconnoiter, while the carrier and the destroyer *Acosta* proceeded as usual. No British planes were aloft, and no initial action was taken to avoid contact. At 4:30, the *Scharnhorst* and *Gneisenau* were battering the *Ardent*, and the destroyer subsequently sank.

continued on page 106

THE NAZI AIRCRAFT CARRIER

Although much has been written about the aircraft carriers of the US, British, and Japanese navies and their combat experience during World War II, far less known is the brief history of the only attempt by Nazi Germany to construct and deploy an aircraft carrier with the Kriegsmarine.

As early as 1933, German naval commanders contemplated the construction of an aircraft carrier displacing twenty-two thousand tons, capable of a top speed of thirty-five knots, and carrying a complement of fifty aircraft, including Messerschmitt Bf 109 fighters, Junkers Ju 87 Stuka dive-bombers, and Fieseler Fi 167 biplanes that carried torpedoes, each adapted for naval service. Plans were approved for the construction of two carriers, initially referred to as A and B. The building of Carrier B proceeded so slowly that it was discontinued in March 1940.

Work on Carrier A, however, proceeded. The keel was laid on December 28, 1936, and two years later the vessel was launched as the *Graf Zeppelin* with an intended complement of 1,760 sailors. Eventually, she was to displace 28,090 tons with an overall length of just over 820 feet and a powerplant of four geared steam turbines that generated two hundred thousand shaft horsepower. Its armament was to include sixteen 5.9-inch guns and more than sixty twenty-millimeter, thirty-millimeter, and forty-millimeter antiaircraft weapons.

With work on the carrier nearing completion in the spring of 1940, however, scarce resources were diverted to the construction of more U-boats to prosecute the Battle of the Atlantic. It was resumed with a modified design in May 1942, and then halted in January 1943, as the Third Reich experienced numerous military reverses. The unfinished carrier was then towed from Kiel to Stettin and scuttled in early 1945 to avoid capture by the advancing Soviet Red Army.

The Soviets refloated the *Graf Zeppelin* in 1946 and attempted to tow the carrier to the port of Leningrad the next year; however, the ship sank en route, probably after striking a floating mine.

The *Graf Zeppelin* was the only aircraft carrier ever to be launched by Germany.

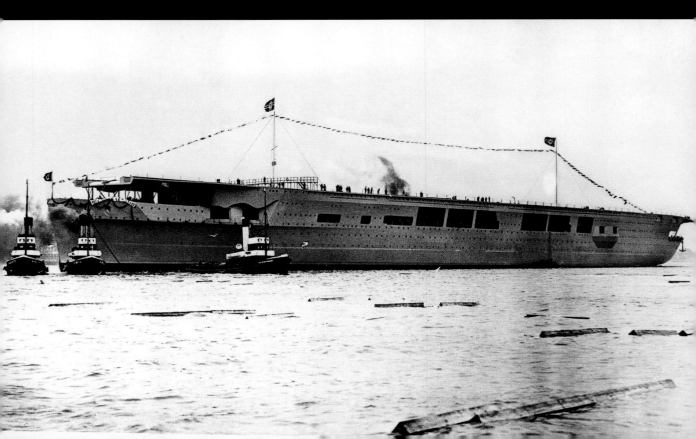

Above: Festooned with garland and a Nazi flag, the aircraft carrier *Graf Zeppelin* awaits launching ceremonies on December 8, 1938. Construction work on the carrier was initiated and halted on more than one occasion, and after World War II the hull of the scuttled warship was refloated by the Soviets. The *Graf Zeppelin* sank for good in 1946, presumably after striking a mine, as the Soviets attempted to tow the hull to the port of Leningrad. © *Sueddeutsche Zeitung Photo/Alamy*

Opposite: After launching, *Graf Zeppelin* floats in the harbor at Kiel surrounded by a trio of attending tugboats. The carrier was expected to displace more than 28,000 tons but was never completed. *National Naval Aviation Museum/Robert L. Lawson Photograph Collection/1996.488.037.060*

Biplanes of the Royal Navy Fleet Air Arm are photographed aboard the HMS *Illustrious*, circa 1938. Although such aircraft were largely obsolete by the beginning of World War II, Fairey Swordfish torpedo bombers flew from the deck of the *Illustrious* on November 11, 1940, and crippled the Italian fleet at its anchorage in the harbor of Taranto. © *Pictorial Press Ltd./Alamy*

continued from page 103

Five minutes later, the British carrier loomed ahead, and the *Scharnhorst* opened fire on the fat, now nearly defenseless target. Immediately the carrier was hit, and one shell smashed into the island above the bridge, killing several men, including the carrier's captain. Another eleven-inch shell tore a large hole in the flight deck and blew apart two Swordfish torpedo planes that were trying to take off. The carrier began to list to starboard, steering was wrecked, and an explosion in the engine room caused a loss of power.

The *Scharnhorst* and *Gneisenau* closed to point-blank range and pounded the carrier, which sank just after 6:00 a.m. The *Acasta* went down a few minutes later. Only forty-three British sailors survived the sinking of the HMS *Glorious*.

As vexing and troublesome as these early encounters had been, British carrier air power did strike a decisive blow in

the autumn of 1940. Italian fascist dictator Benito Mussolini had committed years earlier to the construction of a powerful fleet that would rival the Royal Navy for dominance in the Mediterranean Sea, which Mussolini considered to be an Italian lake.

Although the Royal Navy had pioneered aircraft carrier development, its aircraft remained painfully obsolescent. As war loomed in the summer of 1939, the Fleet Air Arm consisted of only 340 aircraft, virtually all of them antiquated biplanes. Nevertheless, something had to be done about the Italian menace that threatened British operations from Gibraltar to the Middle East and all along the coast of North Africa.

As early as 1935, the Royal Navy had contemplated a preemptive strike against the Italians. When Arthur L. St. George Lyster, rear admiral aircraft carriers Mediterranean, came aboard the brand-new carrier HMS *Illustrious* in the summer of 1940, an existing plan was revived.

At anchor in the port of Taranto in southern Italy, the Italian navy, or Regia Marina, had six battleships, seven heavy cruisers, two light cruisers, and eight destroyers. Formidable though they were, the Italian warships were perhaps more vulnerable in harbor than on the open sea. Lyster and Adm. Andrew Cunningham, commander-in-chief of the Mediterranean Fleet, set the air raid on Taranto, codenamed Operation Judgement, in motion.

After several reconnaissance flights to verify that the Italian warships were still in port, twenty-four Fairey Swordfish torpedo planes, some equipped with aerial torpedoes and others with bombs to create a diversion ashore, lifted off from the deck of the *Illustrious* on the night of November 11, 1940, to attack in two waves.

The first wave consisted of twelve planes, and four of these lost their way in the cloud cover and darkness. Just after 11:00 p.m., Lt. Cmdr. K. W. Williamson, leader of the first wave, flew his Swordfish into the teeth of antiaircraft fire and unleashed a torpedo that blew a hole twenty-seven feet wide below the waterline of the battleship *Conte di Cavour*. Williamson was promptly shot down. The remaining Swordfish of the first wave hit the battleship *Littorio* with two torpedoes. The nine Swordfish of the second wave, led by Lt. Cmdr. J. W. "Ginger" Hale, put another torpedo into the *Littorio* and scored a single torpedo hit on the battleship *Caio Duilio*, which flooded the ship's forward magazines.

The *Conte di Cavour* settled upright on the bottom of the shallow harbor, while both the *Littorio* and *Caio Duilio* were run aground to prevent them from sinking. The cruiser *Trento* was slightly damaged by a bomb that failed to explode. The British lost two Swordfish in the raid on Taranto. Williamson and his observer, Lt. N. J. Scarlett, miraculously survived and were taken prisoner. The pilot and observer of the second torpedo bomber were killed. Williamson and Hale received the Distinguished Service Order, while Scarlett and Hale's observer, Lt. G. A. Carline, accepted the Distinguished Service Cross for the mission.

The Taranto Raid demonstrated the feasibility of a carrier-based air attack against an enemy fleet at anchor. The old Swordfish had trumped Italian air defenses and cut Regia Marina battleship strength in the Mediterranean in half with torpedoes modified to run in the shallow water of the harbor. Senior commanders of the Imperial Japanese Navy took great interest in the raid, which emboldened their planning of the infamous attack on Pearl Harbor the following year.

British Prime Minister Winston Churchill once commented that the U-boat menace to his country's tenuous lifeline of war materiel and vital supplies stretching across thousands of miles of ocean had been the only threat that might be insurmountable during the fight to the death with the Nazis during World War II. The Allies could not declare victory in the Battle of the Atlantic until 1944, and compounding Churchill's concern over the German U-boats was the danger presented by the surface raiders of the Kriegsmarine. From the Arctic Circle to the Indian Ocean, pocket battleships, battlecruisers, and raiders disguised as merchantmen exacted a heavy toll on Allied shipping.

However, the most feared of the raiders were the Nazi battleships *Bismarck* and *Tirpitz*. Eventually British bombers sank the *Tirpitz* at anchor in the harbor of Tromsø, Norway. In the spring of 1941, *Bismarck* and her consort, the heavy cruiser *Prinz Eugen*, sought to break out into the Atlantic. The resulting chase and destruction of the *Bismarck* is an epic of naval warfare, and again the lumbering Fairey Swordfish biplane, flown from an aircraft carrier deck, played a pivotal role.

The forty-two-thousand-ton *Bismarck* carried a main armament of eight fifteen-inch guns mounted in four turrets. Her firepower would be lethal among the merchant ships of an Atlantic convoy, and it was unlikely that any gallant escort could stand up to the big guns of the battleship for long. The Admiralty rushed to bring every available asset to bear in the effort to find and sink the *Bismarck*.

On May 24, after a deadly weeklong game of hide and seek, the German warships sank the battlecruiser HMS *Hood*, pride of the Royal Navy, and damaged the new battleship HMS *Prince of Wales*; fought off an attack launched from the carrier *Victorious*; and disappeared from British radar screens. However, the Nazi battleship was hurt during the fight on May 24. One British shell ruptured a fuel tank, seawater rushed in, and an oil slick trailed the vessel. The damage was significant enough to cause Adm. Günther Lütjens to detach the *Prinz Eugen* and head for the French port of Brest. Soon, he hoped to be in range of German land-based fighters and bombers and within a protective arc of U-boats.

Later, for reasons never fully explained, Lütjens broke radio silence with a long transmission to Berlin, allowing the British to correct an error in course that had them steaming in the wrong direction. On the morning of May 26, a flying boat spotted the *Bismarck* again, moving ever nearer to friendly air cover and the port of Brest. It looked as if the German battleship might make good its escape.

Admiral Sir John Tovey, commander of the British Home Fleet, had one option left. Based at Gibraltar, Force H under Somerville's command had come up from the Mediterranean. It included the aircraft carrier *Ark Royal* and its complement of Swordfish. On the afternoon of May 26, fifteen of the flying anachronisms, affectionately known as "Stringbags," took off from the carrier in search of the *Bismarck*.

Several of the Swordfish mistook the cruiser HMS *Sheffield* for the enemy and attacked, scoring no hits. Those with torpedoes still in their slings continued on, found the *Bismarck*, and struck the great ship with two torpedoes. The damage from one of these was negligible; however, the other jammed the behemoth's rudders, turning it fifteen degrees to port. The damage could not be repaired, and the *Bismarck* was able to steer only one course—northwest toward the pursuing battleships of the Royal Navy.

The following morning, the British battleships *King George V* and *Rodney* pounded the *Bismarck* with fourteen- and sixteen-inch shells. The German battleship blazed from stem to stern and absorbed incredible punishment. The carnage was horrific. Finally, just after 11:00 a.m., the *Bismarck* heeled over to port and sank stern first. Whether torpedoes from the British cruiser *Dorsetshire* (sunk a year later by Japanese planes in the Indian Ocean) or explosives set off by the battleship's own crew were responsible for the coup de grâce is still debated. Only 110 of 2,000 German crewmen survived.

One thing was sure. The ancient Fairey Swordfish and the *Ark Royal* that carried it into battle had gotten the better of the *Bismarck*.

The *Ark Royal*, one of the most famous ships in the history of the Royal Navy, participated not only in the *Bismarck* chase but also the hunt for the German pocket battleship *Graf Spee*, operations in Norway, and the transport of desperately needed fighter planes to embattled Malta. Returning to Gibraltar from one of these ferrying missions on November 13, 1941, the carrier was spotted by the German submarine *U-81*. A single torpedo struck the carrier amidships and tore a gaping hole 130 feet long in its starboard side, causing tremendous flooding. The *Ark Royal* then developed a precipitous list of more than twenty degrees.

Efforts to tow the stricken carrier were fruitless, and the following day the *Ark Royal* capsized, broke in two, and sank. Only one fatality occurred among the ship's complement of nearly 1,500 sailors. Captain Loben Maund, the carrier's commanding officer, was court-martialed and found guilty of negligence in the sinking. However, the *Ark Royal* had also been lost to the single torpedo in part because of its dependence on electric power, knocked out when boilers and other mechanical equipment flooded. With the hard lesson

A biplane with its wings folded rises in the elevator to the flight deck of the HMS *Ark Royal* in early 1941. The *Ark Royal* is probably the most famous Royal Navy aircraft carrier of World War II, having participated in the *Bismarck* chase and in convoy duty to the embattled island of Malta in the Mediterranean. *Popperfoto/Getty Images*

Hit by a single torpedo fired by the German submarine *U-81*, the British aircraft carrier HMS *Ark Royal* lists heavily to starboard on November 13, 1941. Despite efforts to take the carrier under tow to the safety of Gibraltar, the *Ark Royal* sank the following day. The loss of the *Ark Royal* resulted in inquiries, which determined that design flaws contributed to the sinking. © *Pictorial Press Ltd./Alamy*

learned, the design of the *Illustrious*-class carriers then under construction was altered to provide more protection for critical internal spaces.

On August 11, 1942, yet another Royal Navy aircraft carrier fell victim to a German U-boat in the Mediterranean. During the summer, the venerable HMS *Eagle* ferried fighter planes to the island in company with the American carrier *Wasp* and then provided air cover for the heroic transit of the Operation Pedestal convoy to Malta. Assailed from land and sea during an eight-day ordeal, the convoy lost nine merchant

ships. Its escort suffered as well, losing two light cruisers, a destroyer, and the HMS *Eagle* when four torpedoes from the *U-73* ripped into the carrier, which sank in less than four minutes off the coast of the Mediterranean island of Majorca.

With the end of 1942, the aircraft carrier, harbinger of a new kind of naval warfare, had been instrumental in the turning of the tide in favor of the Allies. As World War II dragged on, Allied industrial capacity eclipsed that of their enemies, and among the weapons of war that were responsible for the final victory was the next generation of aircraft carriers.

CARRIER WARFARE REFINED

During the final year of World War I, the British Royal Navy committed to a future that involved the aircraft carrier. With the construction and eventual deployment of the HMS *Argus* after the Armistice, the British acknowledged two things: their wartime experience during the Battle of Jutland revealed that seaborne reconnaissance was inadequate during the run-up to a major surface engagement, and aircraft flying from the decks of carriers could provide far better real-time intelligence on enemy warship deployments.

By the mid-1930s, the Japanese and Italian signatories to the Washington Naval Treaty of 1922 and its successor

A Grumman F6F Hellcat fighter plane prepares for takeoff from the deck of the *Essex*-class aircraft carrier USS Y*orktown*. The halo effect is created by the prop spinning with the aircraft in a stationary position. The corresponding drop in air pressure and the change in temperature create condensation. The halo then moves aft along the fuselage of the plane. *National Archives*

Above: A crewman aboard the *Essex*-class aircraft carrier USS *Yorktown* prepares a bomb for loading on a Grumman TBF Avenger aircraft sitting on the flight deck. The air wing aboard an *Essex*-class carrier exceeded ninety planes, and the combined might of a US Navy task force in World War II sometimes exceeded one thousand aircraft. *National Archives*

Opposite: Pilots of Fighter Squadron VF-16, veterans of aerial combat in the skies above the Marshall Islands, lounge in the ready room of the USS *Lexington* in the autumn of 1943. The *Lexington* was an *Essex*-class carrier commissioned on February 17, 1943, and named in honor of the earlier *Lexington* lost during the Battle of the Coral Sea. The new *Lexington*, nicknamed "the Blue Ghost," participated in numerous operations in the Pacific and survives today as a floating museum in Corpus Christi, Texas. *National Archives*

agreements had begun to jump ship. Totalitarian and militaristic regimes were ascendant, and either overtly or covertly they intended to rearm.

Since the series of agreements had limited aircraft carrier tonnage, the US Navy complied with its carrier designs of the pre–World War II years. In the spring of 1938, the US Congress passed the Naval Expansion Act, which authorized the construction of aircraft carriers totaling forty thousand additional tons. Two carriers were planned, the *Hornet* and the *Essex*. While the *Hornet* achieved quite a degree of fame in its own right, the *Essex* was the progenitor of a now-legendary

class of aircraft carriers. The *Essex*-class carriers, of which twenty-four were eventually completed, became war-winning weapons in the Pacific and symbolized the might of the US Navy for the next half century.

The twenty-seven-thousand-ton *Essex*-class carriers were designed without the treaty restrictions that had shaped the construction of the previous *Yorktown* class and carried on the series of improvements that were initiated with the design of the *Hornet*. With emphasis on offensive capability, particularly the number and types of aircraft the new class could carry, its capacity of more than ninety planes was nearly triple that of

A Grumman F6F Hellcat fighter, its engine roaring in preparation for takeoff, sits on the deck of the USS *Yorktown*, one of twenty-four *Essex*-class carriers eventually completed for the US Navy. *National Naval Aviation Museum/1996.253.7171.001*

contemporary British fleet carriers whose armored flight decks limited their complement of planes to thirty-six.

The beam of each *Essex*-class carrier stretched 93 feet at the waterline and nearly 148 feet at its widest point. The flight deck extended 862 feet, and two centerline elevators measured 48 feet wide and just over 44 feet long. The deck-edge elevator was 60 feet wide and over 34 feet long and could be folded for passage through the locks of the Panama Canal—a direct accommodation for the needs of a two-ocean navy. The *Essex* class outweighed the *Hornet* by 6,500 tons, while its beam was about 10 feet wider. At 872 feet, she was longer by more than 40 feet. As combat aircraft types evolved, the planes themselves became heavier, and design revisions resulted in

the introduction of two flight deck catapults beginning with carriers under construction in March 1943.

Eight Babcock and Wilcox boilers generated steam to four Westinghouse turbines that supplied more than 154,000 horsepower during trials and a top speed of thirty-three knots. Although they were smaller than the early battlecruiser conversion carriers, the *Essex*-class ships delivered size, strike capability, and speed. Hence, they have also come to be known as the "fast" carriers. During World War II, a total of seventeen *Essex*-class carriers were commissioned, and fifteen of them saw action.

The prototype USS *Essex* and two additional carriers of the class were ordered from Newport News Shipbuilding in

Left: Admiral William F. "Bull" Halsey, commander of the US Third Fleet, confers with members of his staff while taking a barge from his flagship, the battleship USS *New Jersey*, to a conference at a base in the Pacific. During operations with Halsey in command, the aircraft carriers and other warships of the US Navy in the Pacific were designated the Third Fleet. The ships were designated the Fifth Fleet while under the command of Adm. Raymond A. Spruance. *National Archives*

Below: The flight deck of the veteran aircraft carrier USS *Enterprise* falls away from a Douglas SBD Dauntless dive-bomber that has just taken off from its deck. The *Enterprise* survived the war and served in company with larger, more advanced carriers. The *Essex*-class aircraft carrier USS *Lexington* is seen in the background at right. *National Archives*

Above: Crewmen busily arm and service Douglas SBD Dauntless dive-bombers aboard the *Essex*-class aircraft carrier USS *Lexington* in November 1943. These activities occurred in support of US Marine Corps operations to capture the islet of Betio at Tarawa Atoll in the Gilbert Islands. The landings at Tarawa were the first Marine Corps amphibious assault against a contested Japanese-held beach during the Pacific War. *National Archives*

Opposite: During flight operations in the Pacific in 1943, a deck crewman waves a checkered flag as the pilot of a Douglas SBD Dauntless dive-bomber prepares to take off from the deck of the *Yorktown*. Other aircraft are lined up to follow on a mission to attack a Japanese base. *National Archives*

Virginia in February 1940. She was laid down on April 28, 1941, and launched on July 31, 1942. At the end of the year, the carrier was commissioned amid a concerted building program that would augment the carrier strength of the US Navy to an unprecedented level. After the United States entered World War II, a total of nineteen more *Essex*-class carriers were steadily ordered during the war years. Carriers were completed at Newport News; the Brooklyn, Philadelphia, and Norfolk navy yards; and the Fore River Shipyard in Massachusetts. During their service lives, various *Essex*-class

carriers underwent substantial upgrades and modifications involving at least five conversion programs.

As World War II progressed, significant design changes occurred during the revision of March 1943. Along with the second flight-deck catapult, additional forty-millimeter antiaircraft mounts were installed in the bow and stern as the flight deck was slightly shortened to allow better fields of fire; vital command spaces such as the CIC (combat information center) and the fighter director position were placed beneath armor protection; clipper bows were installed on the ships

In this photograph taken from the deck of the USS *Essex* on November 13, 1944, the *Independence*-class light carrier USS *Langley* refuels from a fleet tanker in somewhat rough seas. The *Langley* was named in honor of the US Navy's first operational aircraft carrier. Two destroyers are also seen in the image, one of them refueling from the tanker and another approaching the carrier to deliver mail. *National Archives*

then under construction; and safety features were added to the aviation fuel and ventilation systems. The ships completed with the clipper bow have been classified as "long hull," while those with the earlier configuration are referred to as "short hull."

Only one *Essex*-class carrier that was laid down after 1942, the *Bon Homme Richard*, launched in 1944, retained the short hull. However, modifications and improvements were continual during the war years. With improved air defenses, the long hull carriers mounted up to eighteen forty-millimeter guns, and the short hull ships mounted seventeen.

The *Essex*-class aircraft carriers became the sledgehammer of the fast carrier task force concept that was embodied primarily in the organization of Task Force 58 and Task Force 38. As of early 1944, essentially the same US Navy warships were designated the Fifth Fleet (Task Force 58) while under the command of Adm. Raymond A. Spruance, and the Third Fleet (Task Force 38) while under the command of Adm. William F. "Bull" Halsey.

The fast carrier task force came into being in the autumn of 1943 with an arrangement of task groups, each consisting of three to five carriers and a sizable escort of cruisers, destroyers, and the new fast battleships that, unlike older classes, were capable of generating enough speed to maintain formation with the *Essex*-class carriers. In addition to the fleet carriers, the new light carriers of the *Independence* class and the survivors of the prewar designs, the *Enterprise* and *Saratoga*, were operational with the task groups. At any given time more than fifteen US Navy combat aircraft carriers might be operating in the Pacific.

Capt. Truman J. Hedding, who assisted in the outfitting of the *Essex*, recalled:

We knew a lot about flying, and we'd learned a lot about tactics, but we had to learn how to handle more carriers. We realized that never again would the carrier operate in support of the battle line. The fleet would be

PONTIAC

OFFICIAL U. S. NAVY PHOTO

"RIGHT HERE IS WHERE VICTORY STARTS !"

When we at Pontiac Motor Division undertook production of Aircraft Torpedoes, we knew and fully appreciated the manufacturing trials and problems involved. And, we were able to subscribe fully to the words of a high ranking Navy officer who described the Aircraft Torpedo as "the deadliest weapon of the sea, and *the most difficult to make . . .*"

But we fully understood, too, the terrible urgency with which this weapon was needed by our Navy!

That is why Pontiac craftsmen hurled themselves into the job. That is why they responded so willingly to factory bulletin board messages such as the one reproduced above. And that is why, in due time, sleek, slippery and deadly Aircraft Torpedoes began emerging . . . began rolling from our production line.

Yes, Pontiac workmen know that "Right Here Is Where Victory Starts!"—right here

where the weapons of war are being built. But they know *it is only a start!* Our task is simply to build fast and build well, so that courageous men on the firing fronts will have the necessary tools *in volume* and *on time* to *finish the job.* To them goes full credit for the final and glorious Victory ahead!

Every Sunday Afternoon . . . GENERAL MOTORS SYMPHONY OF THE AIR — NBC Network

PONTIAC DIVISION OF GENERAL MOTORS

Oerlikon 20-mm. Anti-Aircraft Cannon

Aircraft Torpedoes for the Navy

40-mm. Automatic Field Guns

Diesel Engine Parts

Axles for M-5 Tanks

Engine Parts for Army Trucks

BUY WAR BONDS

AND STAMPS

Keep America Free!

This dramatic photograph depicts the view from the aircraft elevator of the USS *Saratoga* in November 1943. An SBD Dauntless at right appears to be nosing over the shaft. By now a veteran of the Battle of the Eastern Solomons, the *Saratoga* would go on to play crucial roles at the Marshall Islands, Rabaul, and Iwo Jima. *Library of Congress*

The US Navy's Task Group 38.3 sails in line as it approaches the massive anchorage at Ulithi Atoll in the Caroline Islands after operations against Japanese naval and ground forces in the Philippines. Visible in the photo are the *Independence*-class light aircraft carrier USS *Langley*, the *Essex*-class aircraft carrier *Ticonderoga*, the battleships *North Carolina* and *South Dakota*, and the cruisers *Santa Fe*, *Biloxi*, *Mobile*, and *Oakland*. National Archives

organized around the carriers, and the battleships and cruisers would be primarily for the carriers' protection. So we developed a circular formation . . . with one or two carriers in the center and then another concentric ring of alternating battleships and cruisers that provided tremendous antiaircraft fire. Then outside of that would be a circular screen of destroyers. . . . They provided not only antiaircraft protection, but they provided primarily the submarine protection. Then we came to not only handling just one task group built around two or three carriers, we had two, three, and four task groups. That became quite a potent organization and became the fast carrier force.

The panel of naval officers that developed the concept of the fast carrier task force also devised the tactics for air operations, taking into consideration the position a carrier had to assume to turn into the wind to launch and to recover its planes for air strikes, combat air patrol, and antisubmarine patrol. Two methods, designated Able and

Baker, were determined. The former allowed the carriers to turn individually, and the latter facilitated the movement of the entire group into the wind.

Elaborate procedures were also established for refueling at sea—something akin to planes flying in formation—with the fleet tanker maintaining position and each warship to be refueled making a "pass" so that lines could be extended. The complexity of this wartime combat and logistical choreography grew exponentially as more fast carriers entered service; however, the systems were workable and remarkably few accidents occurred.

Although they were subject to extensive Japanese air attacks during World War II, the fast carriers and their consorts were capable of launching overwhelming air power against the enemy—at times the total number of combat aircraft in service with a task force approached a thousand planes. While US Marine and Army troops conducted amphibious landings on tropical islands and atolls across the Pacific, wresting them from the Japanese one by one while executing the grand strategy called "island hopping," the ships of the US and Allied

THE MAGNIFICENT GRUMMAN HELLCAT

Flying a Grumman F6F Hellcat fighter from the deck of the light carrier USS *Independence* on June 19, 1944, US Navy Lt. (j.g.) Alexander Vraciu shot down six Japanese dive-bombers in the short span of eight minutes during the Battle of the Philippine Sea. When he landed aboard the carrier, Vraciu grinned and held up six fingers to signify the number of victories.

The twenty-five-year-old ace received the Navy Cross and the Distinguished Flying Cross for his exploits and ended the war with nineteen victories. He once remarked of his Hellcat fighter, "These Grummans are beautiful airplanes. If they could cook, I'd marry one." It was a sentiment that was no doubt shared by many other Hellcat pilots in the Pacific.

The Hellcat was deployed to the Pacific in 1943 as a replacement for the earlier F4F Wildcat. Although it had been on the drawing board at the Grumman facility in Bethpage, New York, since 1938, its design was based largely on practical analysis of combat experience against the Japanese Mitsubishi A6M Zero fighter. The Hellcat's predecessor, the Wildcat, had held its own, but the Zero dominated the skies of Asia and the Pacific during the early years of World War II.

However, the Hellcat was representative of a new generation of American fighter plane built to kill the Zero—and in the hands of a skilled pilot that is exactly what it did. Brawny with a weight of more than four and one-half tons and armed with six heavy .50-caliber machine guns, the F6F was powered by a two-thousand-horsepower R-2800 Pratt and Whitney Double Wasp engine. With a top speed of 380 miles per hour and a range that could be extended to 944 miles with auxiliary fuel tanks, the Hellcat was arguably the most formidable carrier-based aircraft of World War II, although pilots who flew the Vought F4U Corsair praised their plane as well.

The appearance of the Hellcat in the skies of the Pacific turned the tide of the air war decidedly in favor of the Allies. During the course of World War II, 307 Hellcat pilots became aces. Pilots flying Hellcats achieved an amazing kill ratio of nineteen to one against the Japanese and shot down nearly 5,200 enemy planes.

A pair of Grumman F6F Hellcat fighters flies on either end of a formation with a Curtiss SB2C Helldiver dive-bomber and a Grumman TBF Avenger torpedo bomber between them. The Hellcat was a powerful fighter, armed with six .50-caliber machine guns and designed specifically to counter the nimble Japanese Mitsubishi A6M Zero fighter that had dominated the skies in the early months of World War II in the Pacific. *National Archives*

navies engaged in the destruction of the Imperial Japanese Navy, particularly its carrier air power, and then the capability of its surface assets and submarines to wage war.

The Battle of the Philippine Sea, the largest carrier-versus-carrier battle in naval history, occurred during American operations to secure the Marianas island chain in the spring of 1944. Admiral Spruance's Task Force 58 formed in five task groups consisting of seven fleet carriers, eight light carriers, seven battleships, eight heavy cruisers, thirteen light cruisers, fifty-eight destroyers, and 956 carrier-based aircraft opposed the Japanese Mobile Fleet under Adm. Jisaburō Ozawa with three large carriers, four light carriers, five battleships, thirteen heavy cruisers, six light cruisers, and twenty-seven destroyers. The Japanese mustered approximately 750 carrier- and land-based planes.

Spruance was initially given the dual charge of covering the land operations to capture the island of Saipan while destroying the Japanese carriers should the opportunity arise. However, the Japanese spotted the American carriers first, and on the morning of June 19, 1944, the Battle of the Philippine Sea began in earnest. Repeated Japanese air raids, launched from land bases on the island of Guam and from the decks of their carriers, were intercepted and decimated by American fighters, particularly the superb Grumman F6F Hellcat, which joined the fleet in 1943. The day's air combat was so one-sided that it came to be known among American pilots as the Great Marianas Turkey Shoot.

For the loss of 350 aircraft, the Japanese managed just a single bomb hit on the battleship USS *South Dakota* that day. Only thirty American planes were shot down or lost in operational accidents.

Admiral Ozawa was aboard the *Taihō*, the largest and newest aircraft carrier in the Japanese fleet. She displaced 30,250 tons with a length of 855 feet, a flight deck just over 843 feet long, and a top speed of more than thirty-three knots with 160,000 shaft horsepower supplied by four Kampon steam turbines and eight boilers, and a complement of sixty-five aircraft. The *Taihō* was ordered in 1939, built by Kawasaki at the shipyards in the city of Kobe, and commissioned on March 7, 1944. It had been the first carrier constructed under Japan's unrealized Modified Fleet Replenishment Program approved in 1942. The design was based on the earlier *Shōkaku*, and four more were ordered but never built. Fifteen carriers based on the *Hiryū* design were also foreseen, but only three were finished. The *Taihō* was the first Japanese aircraft carrier with an armored flight deck and was designed to withstand multiple torpedo or bomb hits and remain operational.

Early on the morning of June 19, the submarine USS *Albacore* spotted the *Taihō*, and as the Japanese carrier completed the launching of forty-two planes in its second raid of the day the submarine fired a spread of six torpedoes. Four of these

Commander David McCampbell, the highest ranking fighter ace in the history of the US Navy with thirty-four confirmed aerial victories, smiles broadly from the cockpit of his Grumman F6F Hellcat fighter aboard the USS *Essex*. At the time this photograph was taken, McCampbell had recorded thirty victories, as documented by the Rising Sun decals emblazoned on the fuselage of his fighter. At the Great Marianas Turkey Shoot, he shot down five Japanese bombers, achieving "ace in a day" status (a feat he achieved twice). McCampbell received the Medal of Honor, Navy Cross, and Silver Star for his service, retired with the rank of captain, and died at the age of eighty-six in 1996. *National Archives*

Shredded by effective antiaircraft fire, a Japanese plane billows smoke and flames as it streaks toward the water during the Battle of the Philippine Sea. The aircraft was shot down during an attack on the escort carrier *Kitkun Bay*. *National Archives*

Above: A significant improvement over the obsolete torpedo bombers in service with the US Navy at the beginning of World War II, the Grumman TBF Avenger became the frontline aircraft of the type after 1942. In this photo, Avengers based at Naval Air Station, Norfolk, Virginia, practice torpedo runs in November of that year. *National Archives*

Right: Grumman TBF Avenger torpedo bombers take an aircraft carrier's elevator to the flight deck to prepare for takeoff. With a crew of three, the Avenger entered service with the US Navy in 1942, and a few were present during the Battle of Midway. Armed with one .50-caliber and two .30-caliber machine guns for defense against enemy fighters, the Avenger was capable of a top speed of 275 miles per hour with a range of one thousand miles. *National Archives*

ran off course. A Japanese pilot who had just taken off bravely sacrificed himself by diving his plane into the fifth torpedo.

The sixth torpedo, however, ran hot and true, blasting a hole in the starboard side of the *Taihō* and rupturing a pair of large tanks filled with aviation fuel. Although it appeared for a while that the *Taihō* would survive, the new carrier became the victim of her crew's inept damage control. At midafternoon, a junior officer opened the ship's ventilation system hoping to

clear the fumes from the leaking aviation fuel. The dangerous vapor spread throughout the carrier, and a single spark from an electric generator ignited a series of catastrophic explosions. As the carrier's brief three-month combat career ended, 1,650 of its 2,150-man crew went with her to the bottom of the Pacific.

Around noon on June 19, the submarine USS *Cavalla* fired six torpedoes at the veteran fleet carrier *Shōkaku*. Three of these hit the carrier's starboard side, rupturing fuel tanks and setting

None but the finest ... with a Vengeance!

WHEN the pilot of this Vultee Vengeance goes upstairs, he's invading disputed territory—*hotly* disputed by Messerschmitts, Focke-Wulfs and hornet-y little Zeros. Naturally, he wants to be sure that everything about his ship is in perfect condition; the motor most of all. It must keep turning over. The success of his mission—his very life—depends on it.

All over the world in this war there are Allied fighting men whose lives depend on their motors. These vital motors need oil that will keep right on providing essential lubrication, in the longest pulls and in the hottest spots.

It is our good fortune that our planes enjoy the advantage of such oils. Neither by plunder nor by discovery in synthetics has the Axis been able to provide anything to equal the quality of these oils.

For there is only one place in all the world where the *best* crude oil is found—the Pennsylvania oil field. And, in Quaker State's four great modern refineries this oil is processed with skill and care to make the finest oils that money can buy—oils with that "Pennsylvania Plus."

In these war days especially, you'll find it pays to give the motor in your car the finest protective lubrication. Infrequent driving increases rather than lessens the need for such care. So drive in for Quaker State Motor Oil and Quaker State Superfine Lubricants wherever you see the green-and-white Quaker State service sign — Quaker State Oil Refining Corporation, Oil City, Pennsylvania.

QUAKER STATE MOTOR OIL
CERTIFIED — GUARANTEED
Retail price 35¢ per quart

OIL IS AMMUNITION—USE IT WISELY

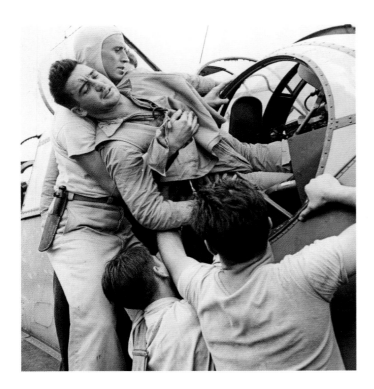

Above left: Following an air raid on the Japanese forward base at Rabaul in the Solomon Islands in November 1943, crewmen aboard the aircraft carrier USS *Saratoga* lift wounded naval aviator Kenneth Bratton from the turret of a Grumman TBF Avenger. *National Archives*

Above right: Admiral Marc Mitscher gazes from the bridge of the USS *Lexington* during the Battle of the Philippine Sea. Mitscher, an aviator and 1910 graduate of the US Naval Academy, exerted operational command of the fast carrier task forces that defeated Japan during World War II in the Pacific while Admirals William F. "Bull" Halsey and Raymond A. Spruance alternated in overall command. Mitscher was responsible for formulating much of the fast carriers' operational doctrine. *National Archives*

off explosions among planes that were being rearmed and refueled on the hangar deck. Exploding ordnance doomed the *Shōkaku*, which sank soon afterward, taking the lives of nearly 1,300 sailors and airmen.

On June 20, Spruance was anxious after sailing westward through the night. Due to the great expanse of ocean separating the opposing forces, American scout planes did not locate the Japanese until after 3:00 p.m. Daylight would be fading soon, but after absorbing a full day of Japanese air attacks on June 19 and remaining relatively unscathed, Spruance followed the second component of his dual order and retaliated. A total of 240 planes were launched in the late afternoon, and though a follow-up strike was canceled as the sun began to sink in the west, the first strike group was not recalled.

Just prior to sunset, the American planes found their targets. Four Grumman TBF Avenger torpedo bombers from the *Independence*-class light carrier *Belleau Wood* hit the 23,770-ton carrier *Hiyō*, converted from an ocean liner and commissioned on July 31, 1942, with bombs and torpedoes. In the fading light, the *Hiyō* sank stern first with the loss of 250 personnel. The veteran carrier *Zuikaku*, the last survivor of the

Pearl Harbor attack nearly three years earlier, and the light carriers *Junyō* and *Chiyoda*, were damaged by bombs.

The Americans lost twenty planes to Japanese antiaircraft fire and fighters. For those that remained, a harrowing flight in the dark to find the carriers of Task Force 58 followed. With fuel gauges neared empty, some pilots were forced to ditch in the sea and others crashed, but some actually succeeded in nocturnal landings aboard any friendly carrier deck they could find.

In a heroic effort to assist the returning pilots, Adm. Marc Mitscher, the Task Force 58 carrier commander, issued a famous order: "Turn on the lights!" The carriers turned their searchlights skyward to provide homing beacons for the pilots flying in total darkness. Eighty planes were lost that night, but many of the pilots and crewmen who had ditched were plucked from the ocean during the next forty-eight hours. Mitscher had taken a tremendous risk, silhouetting his carriers for any Japanese submarine that might be lurking nearby, but his action no doubt saved lives and endeared him to the airmen of Task Force 58.

In retrospect, Spruance had certainly been cautious at the Battle of the Philippine Sea. He was roundly criticized in some naval quarters for not delivering an overwhelming

US Navy escort carriers participate in maneuvers in January 1944. This shot, taken from aft of USS *Manila Bay*, shows, from front to back, USS *Coral Sea*, USS *Corregidor*, USS *Natoma Bay*, and USS *Nassau*. *National Archives*

knockout blow to the Japanese carriers, and there were demands that he be relieved. However, Spruance was the hero of the Battle of Midway, and his superiors—Adm. Chester Nimitz, commander-in-chief Pacific, and Adm. Ernest J. King, chief of naval operations—supported him. The Japanese had lost three aircraft carriers and more than six hundred carrier- and land-based planes. The offensive air capability of the Imperial Japanese Navy had been broken for good.

In response to the critical need for aircraft carriers in the opening months of World War II, construction of the *Essex*-class fleet carriers had been accelerated. Along with the fleet carriers came the light carriers of the *Independence* class and

several classes of small escort carriers to shoulder the burden of US Navy operations in both the Atlantic and Pacific.

Built on the hulls of *Cleveland*-class light cruisers, nine *Independence*-class carriers displacing eleven thousand tons and carrying more than forty planes each were completed between January and November 1943. More than 622 feet long with a beam of just over 109 feet, the *Independence*-class carriers were powered by boilers and turbines that generated one hundred thousand shaft horsepower and a top speed of nearly thirty-two knots. Due to their emergency conversions from light cruiser hulls, the light carriers were considered less than optimal in their new roles, often pitching in heavy seas

continued on page 133

Stills from a 1943 US Navy training film offer a glimpse of work and hazards aboard a World War II carrier. At top left, a flight deck officer signals that aircraft are ready to commence operations, while the arresting gear crewman in green cap and jersey at upper right checks a cable. At lower left, fueling crews tried to refill aircraft as soon as possible after landing. "Hot pappas" in asbestos suits, lower right, were charged with extracting flight crews from crashed aircraft.
National Archives

Left: The partially visible "No Smoking" sign seems like sound advice as rockets and bombs aboard the escort carrier USS *Santee* await loading on aircraft for operations on Okinawa, Ishigaki, and Saka Shima in April 1945. *Santee* was launched in 1939 as a commercial oil hauler and then purchased by the US Navy and converted to a carrier in 1942. *National Archives*

Below: An SB2C Helldiver dive-bomber circles for landing on the USS *Yorktown* in July 1944. The Helldiver was included in the standard complement of seventy-two aircraft aboard *Essex*-class carriers such as the *Yorktown*. *US Navy photo*

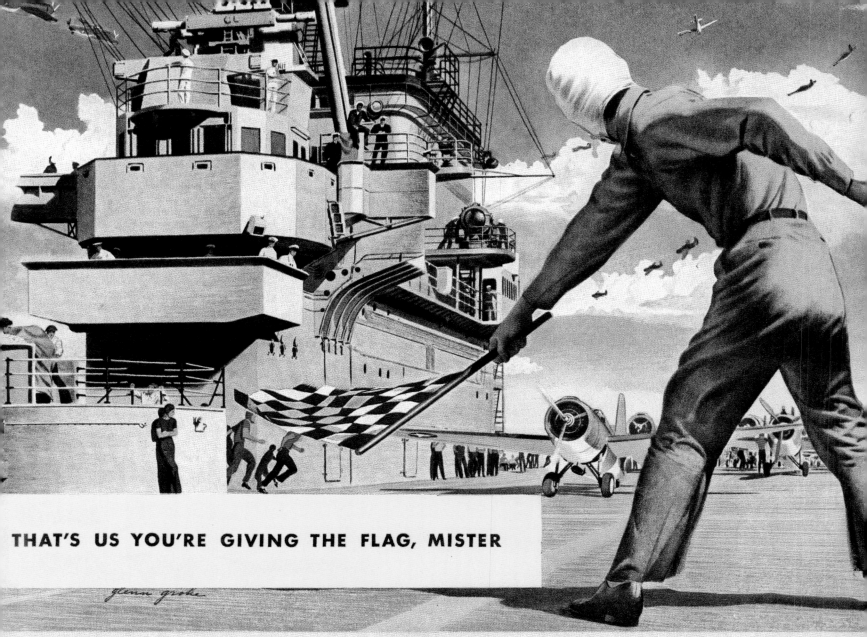

THAT'S US YOU'RE GIVING THE FLAG, MISTER

glenn grohe

If you're a manufacturer, and would like 25" x 38" enlargements of this page, for posting in your plant, with all space below illustration left blank for your own message: write Aluminum Company of America, 1999 Gulf Bldg., Pittsburgh, Pa

So much of that *Wildcat* . . . ninety percent anyway . . . went through our hands, it seems like we were standing right there beside you. We had our hands on her wings first when they were just dirt in the ground. We dug and we smelted; we rolled and we forged. And we're working three shifts a day, eight days a week to turn the shining metal over to the plane and engine builders, quick. Mister, this one outfit of ours is making aluminum for your planes faster right now than any one whole country ever made it before. And you haven't heard the half of what we've got under way. Give her the flag, Mister. We're making aluminum like nobody's business.

The men and women of ALCOA ALUMINUM

Above: *Casablanca*-class escort carrier USS *Shipley Bay*, her camouflage still pristine, anchors at Majuro Atoll in the Marshall Islands in May 1944, just two months after commissioning. The *Casablanca*-class represented the most numerous type of carrier during World War II, with fifty commissioned from 1942 to 1944. Escort carriers were slow and more lightly armed and armored than the much larger fleet carriers, but they could be built quickly and in large numbers. *US Navy photo*

Left: The escort carrier USS *Bogue* lies at anchor off Bermuda in February 1945. The "Jeep" carriers of the *Bogue*-class displaced 9,800 tons and carried up to twenty-four aircraft. These warships were introduced in an antisubmarine role as convoy escorts and to provide air cover and support for troops during amphibious operations in the Pacific. The majority of the 120 escort carriers built for the navy during World War II were of the *Bogue* and *Casablanca* classes. *National Naval Aviation Museum/Robert L. Lawson Photograph Collection/1996.488.032.015*

continued from page 129
and challenging even for experienced pilots as platforms from which to take off and land.

The escort carriers were developed to provide air cover to merchant convoy escort forces and to hunter-killer groups that patrolled the surface of the Atlantic in search of German U-boats, protecting the convoys and often turning the tables on the would-be attackers. They also provided air cover for amphibious landing operations and direct support for ground troops in the Pacific Theater. Known affectionately as "jeep carriers" and "baby flattops" to the Americans, and as "Woolworth carriers" among sailors of the British Royal Navy, the escort carriers were highly successful in the antisubmarine role. More than 120 escort carriers were built in US shipyards

during World War II, and the largest numbers belonged to the *Casablanca* and *Bogue* classes.

The *Bogue*-class carriers displaced 9,800 tons and began entering service in 1942 with up to twenty-four aircraft aboard. They were 495 feet long with a beam of 69 feet and a top speed of eighteen knots. A total of forty-five were launched, and thirty-four of these served with the Royal Navy after redesignation as the *Attacker* and *Ruler* classes.

The smaller *Casablanca*-class escort carriers entered service in 1943 and were developed on the recommendation of shipping magnate Henry Kaiser, father of the Liberty and Victory cargo ships that were mass produced during the war. Built on modified merchant ship hulls, the *Casablanca* class

Planes from Air Group 15 aboard the carrier USS *Essex* score a direct hit on the Japanese battleship *Ise* during the Battle of Leyte Gulf on October 25, 1944. The Battle of Leyte Gulf was actually a series of engagements fought around the Philippines during the invasion of the island of Leyte, and Adm. William F. Halsey has been criticized for taking his fast battleships and fleet carriers well north of the invasion area in pursuit of a Japanese decoy force. *National Archives*

carried twenty-seven aircraft and displaced 7,800 tons with a length of 512 feet, a beam of just over 65 feet, and a top speed of eighteen knots. Fifty of the class were completed, and all served with the US Navy.

In October 1944, Gen. Douglas MacArthur made good on his promise to return to the Philippines. American troops poured ashore on the Philippine island of Leyte, and the US Navy was again deployed in force. Four months after the victory at the Battle of the Philippine Sea, Task Force 38 was at sea under the command of Admiral Halsey.

At this stage of the Pacific War, American industrial capacity had far outstripped that of the Japanese, and Halsey led a core of eight fleet carriers and eight light carriers while Adm. Thomas C. Kinkaid's Seventh Fleet included eighteen escort carriers that would cover the Leyte landing beaches. Between them, the two US fleets were escorted by a dozen

battleships, twenty-four heavy and light cruisers, and scores of destroyers.

The Japanese had drawn contingency plans for an American offensive in either the Philippines or against Formosa. The Philippine plan, called Shō-Gō One, included a carrier force under Admiral Ozawa along with two additional surface squadrons. With few aircraft and virtually no experienced pilots, Ozawa's carriers posed little real threat to the Leyte landings. However, the hope was that they might be sufficient bait to lure Halsey away from his distant coverage position off Leyte since the destruction of Japanese carriers remained a high priority for the US Navy. Their plan was helped by the fact that the pugnacious Halsey was always spoiling for a fight.

If Ozawa's northern force were successful in luring Task Force 38 with its fleet carriers and fast battleships away from Leyte, the two powerful Japanese surface forces might attack the American transports off the Leyte beachhead and destroy the amphibious operation, dealing a heavy blow to the American offensive timetable in the Pacific. Two surface squadrons under Adms. Kiyohide Shima and Shōji Nishimura, composed of old battleships and cruisers, constituted the Japanese southern force approaching Leyte through Surigao Strait.

The Japanese center force under Adm. Takeo Kurita would approach Leyte via the San Bernardino Strait. With Kurita were the super battleships *Yamato* and *Musashi* (the heaviest battleships ever built and mounting eighteen-inch guns) as well as three smaller battleships, ten heavy cruisers, two light cruisers, and fifteen destroyers. One Japanese staff officer remarked that if Shō-Gō One succeeded, Kurita would fall upon the defenseless American transports off Leyte like "a hawk among chickens."

The resulting Battle of Leyte Gulf, fought from October 23 to October 26, 1944, may be viewed as four separate naval engagements. Collectively, the battle is recognized as the largest naval engagement in history and a victory for the US Navy despite a brush with disaster. On the night of October 23, Kurita's center force was attacked by American submarines, which sank two cruisers and damaged a third. Kurita pressed on, and the following day relentless air attacks launched from the fleet carriers *Essex*, *Intrepid*, *Lexington*, *Franklin*, and the veteran *Enterprise*, along with the light carrier *Cabot*, hit the *Musashi* with at least seventeen bombs and nineteen torpedoes, sinking the great warship.

While American carrier planes struck the Japanese center force, the enemy countered with three waves of land-based bombers from the Philippine island of Luzon that headed for the American carriers near Leyte. Hellcat fighter pilots shot down many of the incoming planes, but shortly after 9:30 a.m. a single Japanese Yokosuka D4Y3 "Judy" dive-bomber slipped through and dropped a 551-pound bomb that penetrated the flight deck of the light carrier *Princeton* between its two elevators. For a time it appeared that the carrier would survive, but internal explosions wracked the ship, which was eventually sunk by torpedoes from an American cruiser. The *Princeton* was the only *Independence*-class carrier lost to enemy action during World War II.

Late in the afternoon of October 24, American search aircraft finally spotted Ozawa's northern force. Halsey mistakenly believed that Kurita's center force was retiring after the drubbing it had received from the air earlier in the day, and hastily he issued orders to begin a pursuit of Ozawa toward Cape Engaño to the north. A series of miscommunications resulted in the heavy warships under Halsey steaming away from their Leyte coverage positions just as the Japanese had envisioned. Left all alone were the escort carriers, destroyers,

During the Battle of Leyte Gulf, a Japanese aircraft carrier is bracketed by bombs and takes at least one direct hit from planes of Air Group 15 based aboard the carrier USS *Essex*. Although the planes of Adm. William F. Halsey's fast carriers inflicted heavy damage on the decoy force led by Adm. Jisaburō Ozawa at Leyte Gulf, the landing and supply area around the beaches of Leyte was left dangerously exposed. *National Archives*

and destroyer escorts of Task Group 77.4, divided into three separate units designated Taffy 1, Taffy 2, and Taffy 3 under the command of Adm. Clifton A. F. Sprague.

Contrary to Halsey's assumption, Kurita had continued steaming toward the Leyte beachhead. At 3:00 p.m. on October 25, his remaining battleships and cruisers emerged from San Bernardino Strait. Soon they encountered Sprague's unarmored baby flattops and their little escorts off the island of Samar.

The Battle off Samar, one of the great David and Goliath fights in naval history, ensued. Kurita's ships fired heavy shells, some of which passed through the thin skins of the escort carriers without exploding. The small contingent of available aircraft strafed and made dummy bomb and torpedo runs against the big Japanese ships, and the gallant destroyers and destroyer escorts charged to the defense of the carriers. During the unequal battle, heavy-caliber shells pummeled the escort carrier *Gambier Bay*, which sank along with the destroyers *Johnston* and *Hoel* and the destroyer escort *Samuel B. Roberts*. The destroyer *Heermann* survived with heavy damage.

The ferocity of the American defense off Samar convinced Kurita that he was facing a much stronger force than was actually confronting him—possibly even Halsey's fleet carriers

Above left: Admiral Takeo Kurita was given command of the powerful Japanese center force during the Battle of Leyte Gulf. Although the Japanese plan was successful in luring the modern battleships and aircraft carriers of Adm. William F. Halsey's Third Fleet northward, Kurita lost his nerve when confronted by stiff resistance from small destroyers, destroyer escorts, and escort carriers during the Battle off Samar on October 25, 1944, and chose to retire rather than proceed to bombard the supply vessels and landing beaches on the Philippine island of Leyte. Kurita died in 1977 at the age of eighty-eight. *National Archives*

Above right: Hit by antiaircraft fire from a nearby Navy ship, a Japanese kamikaze suicide plane flips sideways before narrowly missing its intended target, the escort carrier USS *Sangamon*. The first kamikaze attacks encountered by the US Navy during the Pacific War occurred during the Battle of Leyte Gulf. *National Archives*

and battleships. With victory in his grasp, the Japanese admiral ordered his ships to retire. As the Japanese turned back, one American sailor exclaimed, "Dammit boys, they're getting away!" Miraculously, the Taffy ships had held the line.

On October 25, Halsey's carrier planes attacked Ozawa's decoy force in the Battle of Cape Engaño, finally exacting vengeance for Pearl Harbor on the carrier *Zuikaku* and sinking the light carriers *Chitose* and *Zuihō*. On the same day, the American escort carrier *St. Lo* was sunk off Leyte by a new and frightening weapon: the kamikaze suicide plane. It was a foretaste of the devastation to be wrought by the kamikaze during the coming months.

On the night of October 25, Adm. Jesse Oldendorf commanded an American task force led by six battleships in the destruction of the Japanese southern force during the Battle of Surigao Strait. Five of the battleships—*West Virginia*, *Tennessee*, *California*, *Pennsylvania*, and *Maryland*—had been repaired and modernized after being sunk or damaged at Pearl

Harbor. The sixth battleship, USS *Mississippi*, fired the last salvo in history between heavy surface warships. It was the end of an era.

Despite the positive outcome at Leyte Gulf, Halsey was heavily criticized for his decision to pursue Ozawa amid a tangle of missed or misinterpreted orders that should have prevented the near debacle off Samar. Halsey vigorously defended his actions, but his conduct remains a source of controversy.

As World War II progressed, Japanese industrial capacity was severely hampered by American submarines that sank merchant ships and by increasingly heavy bombing raids launched from bases in the Marianas. Strapped for resources and raw materials, the Imperial Navy had nevertheless begun the construction of a third super battleship in the spring of 1940. However, after the disastrous defeat and the loss of four aircraft carriers at Midway, the order was given to convert the hull to a new super aircraft carrier. The sixty-six-thousand-ton *Shinano* was launched on October 8, 1944, with a capacity

continued on page 140

Above: The Japanese light carrier *Zuihō*, its flight deck painted with an intricate camouflage scheme, maneuvers while under attack by planes from the USS *Enterprise* during the Battle of Cape Engaño, which was part of the larger Battle of Leyte Gulf, on October 25, 1944. The *Zuihō*, and another light carrier, the *Chitose*, were sunk along with the fleet carrier *Zuikaku*, the last survivor of the Pearl Harbor attack. *National Archives*

Left: The final moments of the *Zuikaku* are captured in this dramatic photo. The carrier lists heavily as sailors salute. The *Zuikaku* was the last of the Japanese carriers that had participated in the attack on Pearl Harbor in 1941. *National Naval Aviation Museum/Robert L. Lawson Photograph Collection/1996.488.258.009*

Above: Its stern awash from damage delivered by American carrier-based aircraft, a Japanese warship trails debris in the waters off the Philippine island of Leyte in late 1944. The US Navy victory in the Battle of Leyte Gulf virtually destroyed the remaining offensive capability of the Imperial Japanese Navy in World War II. *National Archives*

Opposite: Smoke billows from the flight deck of the *Independence*-class light carrier *Belleau Wood* after a kamikaze crashed into its flight deck among parked aircraft off the coast of the Philippines on October 30, 1944. The fleet carrier USS *Franklin*, also hit by a kamikaze, belches smoke in the distance. *National Archives*

Left: Japanese Admiral Kiyohide Shima led his small task force to destruction during the Battle of Surigao Strait. A component of the Battle of Leyte Gulf, the action in Surigao Strait was one-sided as US Navy battleships and other warships under the command of Adm. Jesse Oldendorf blocked the strait and destroyed the oncoming Japanese warships on the night of October 24–25, 1944. Shima survived the debacle and died in 1973 at the age of eighty-three. *National Archives*

As antiaircraft fire laces the sky, a Japanese kamikaze pilot flying a Mitsubishi A6M Zero armed with a bomb screams downward toward the USS *Lexington* on November 5, 1944. The resulting fire was under control in less than half an hour, and the carrier resumed flight operations. *National Archives*

Fires burn aboard the USS *Essex* after a kamikaze struck the edge of the flight deck on November 25, 1944, and destroyed several planes that had been readied for flight operations. Fifteen men were killed and forty-four wounded. This photo was taken from the deck of the carrier USS *Ticonderoga*. *National Archives*

continued from page 136

of forty-seven aircraft and the capability to transport rocket-propelled *Ohka* suicide bombs and small *Shin'yō* suicide boats.

Although the *Shinano* was expected to achieve a top speed of twenty-seven knots with a powerplant of boilers and steam turbines that delivered 150,000 horsepower, the carrier never reached that during trials. On November 29, 1944, the mammoth warship was en route from the Yokosuka shipyards to the naval base at Kure for continued construction. The submarine USS *Archerfish* stalked the *Shinano* for several hours before firing a spread of six torpedoes. Four struck the carrier on her starboard side, causing severe flooding. A substantial list developed, and inexperienced damage-control parties performed poorly.

Eight hours after the *Archerfish* attacked, the *Shinano* capsized and sank. Postwar analysis of the episode revealed that the carrier suffered from serious design flaws, particularly in its defenses against torpedo hits. This, coupled with the inexperience and overconfidence of the ship's crew, was a recipe for disaster. US intelligence could not confirm the existence of the *Shinano* until after the war, doubting the claim of Cmdr. Joseph F. Enright, skipper of the *Archerfish*, that he had sunk the behemoth. Subsequently, Enright was awarded the Navy Cross.

Steady American progress across the Pacific continued into 1945. The strategically important island of Iwo Jima fell to

US Marines in March after thirty-four days of bitter fighting. On April 1, a curious double observance of Easter Sunday and April Fools' Day, US troops landed on the island of Okinawa, just 340 miles from the Japanese main islands.

The struggle to secure Okinawa lasted eighty-three days and presented the US Navy with its sternest test of the carrier war in the Pacific. While fighting raged on land, the navy was obliged to keep station offshore and support the effort.

In desperation, the Japanese intensified their kamikaze air attacks. Vice Admiral Matome Ugaki, commander of the Fifth Air Fleet, organized massed kamikaze raids against the US ships in ten waves that were known euphemistically as *Kikusui*, or "floating chrysanthemums." Altogether, Ugaki hurled nearly 4,500 suicide planes at the enemy. Twenty-nine American ships were sunk and another 120 damaged. During the course

In this photo nicknamed "Murderer's Row," the strength of the US Navy in the Pacific is revealed as six *Essex*-class aircraft carriers ride at anchor at Ulithi Atoll in the Caroline Islands. From the foreground into the distance are the USS *Wasp*, USS *Yorktown*, USS *Hornet*, USS *Hancock*, USS *Ticonderoga*, and USS *Lexington*. This image was taken in December 1944 from a plane of the *Ticonderoga* air group. *National Archives*

On the morning of March 19, 1945, the USS *Franklin* was hit by two bombs from a single Japanese plane while conducting flight operations approximately forty-five miles off the coast of Japan. At the time the bombs struck, thirty-one armed and fueled aircraft were being readied for takeoff. Fires raged aboard the carrier, and ordnance exploded. Although no *Essex*-class carriers were lost to enemy action during World War II, the *Franklin* was the most heavily damaged. This image was taken from the deck of the cruiser USS *Santa Fe. National Archives*

The USS *Essex* is pictured off the island of Okinawa in the spring of 1945. The aircraft carriers of the *Essex*-class were the first constructed for the US Navy without treaty restrictions. Displacing twenty-seven thousand tons, these fleet carriers projected air power across the Pacific during World War II. *National Archives*

of the battle, 1,500 Japanese suicide pilots perished, while 3,048 American naval personnel died and more than 6,000 were wounded.

The Japanese also sent the super battleship *Yamato* on a one-way suicide voyage against the US Navy. On April 7, American carrier planes swarmed around the giant warship like angry bees. Planes from eight carriers, including the fleet carriers *Hornet* and *Bennington* and the light carriers *Belleau Wood* and *San Jacinto* of Task Group 58.1—as well as the fleet carriers *Essex*, *Bunker Hill*, and *Hancock* and the light carrier *Bataan* of Task Group 58.3—attacked the *Yamato* in successive waves from just after 12:30 in the afternoon. Hit by at least a dozen torpedoes and as many bombs, the *Yamato* was ripped by a huge explosion as she capsized and sank about two hours later.

American destroyers, destroyer escorts, and other vessels manning an early-warning picket line suffered tremendously

under the rain of Ugaki's kamikazes. Nor were the American aircraft carriers immune from attack. On the morning of May 11, the fifty-eighth day of the battle, the *Essex*-class carrier *Bunker Hill*, flagship of Admiral Mitscher, came under attack during the sixth Kikusui. Most of these suicide planes were shot down by US fighters and antiaircraft guns, but two Mitsubishi Zeros slipped through the protective umbrella.

Just after 10:00 a.m., Lt. (j.g.) Yasunori Seizō followed his 551-pound bomb into thirty-four armed and fueled aircraft sitting on the *Bunker Hill*'s flight deck. The bomb smashed through the teakwood decking, exited the other side of the ship, and exploded in midair, while the remnants of Seizō's Zero careened across the flight deck and over the side. Moments later,

continued on page 146

The stress of combat is evident in the face of a crewman aboard a US Navy aircraft carrier as his forty-millimeter gun mount engages targets during feverish action in the Pacific. The forty-millimeter Bofors antiaircraft gun was one of the finest weapons of its type in service during World War II. Originally configured as a single-barreled weapon, it was later manufactured in a twin mount and proved most effective. *National Archives*

U. S. AIRCRAFT CARRIERS not only carry *more* gasoline than any service station ashore, but they also carry *better* gasoline.

Every drop of gasoline used by our fighting carrier planes is the highest octane fuel made by oil companies in America. All of these companies use Ethyl fluid to improve their aviation gasoline.

Since the Army and Navy must have millions of gallons of this 100 octane fuel, government agencies have had to place limits on the quantity and quality of gasoline for civilian use. But—when the fighting is over you'll get better gasoline than ever before.

ETHYL CORPORATION

Chrysler Building
New York 17, N. Y.

In this photo taken from the deck of the *Essex*-class aircraft carrier USS *Wasp*, a Japanese plane hit by antiaircraft fire from the fleet carrier *Bunker Hill* and the light carrier USS *Cabot* plunges toward the Pacific. The kamikaze suicide planes that began attacking ships of the US Navy in late 1943 inflicted serious damage and sank numerous vessels. *National Archives*

continued from page 143

twenty-two-year-old Ens. Kiyoshi Ogawa released his bomb and then slammed into the carrier's flight deck near the island.

In an instant, the *Bunker Hill* was an inferno. Mitscher lost half his staff and barely escaped. Thirty pilots were sitting below in the ready room and rushed into a neighboring corridor, where they smothered as the nearby fires consumed all available oxygen. The photographic image of their bodies lying jumbled together is one of the most poignant of World War II.

Extensive damage-control training paid off—the fires were brought under control and the still-seaworthy *Bunker Hill* began the arduous, seven-thousand-mile voyage to the Puget Sound Navy Yard in Washington State. Three hundred seventy-three men died aboard the carrier, while another 263 were wounded and 43 were declared missing.

The long reach of the US Navy in the spring of 1945 stretched to within a few minutes' flight time of the Japanese home islands. On March 19, twelve days before the Okinawa landings, the *Essex*-class aircraft carrier USS *Franklin* was one of several conducting air strikes against Japanese bases, intent on neutralizing any threat enemy planes might pose to the Okinawa operation.

"The mission of our task force was to raid the Japanese airfields in Kyushu, Shikoku, and western Honshu, from which we expected all the Japanese aircraft would be launched against the Okinawa invasion, and, in truth, that's what happened," explained Capt. Stephen Jurika, Jr., the navigator aboard the *Franklin*. "The launch point for our aircraft was forty-five miles off the mainland of Honshu. It would take our fighters and bombers somewhere between twenty and thirty minutes from time of launch to arrive at enemy airfields."

As with other carriers in task group 58.2, the *Franklin*'s flight deck was periodically packed with aircraft that were fueled and ready for takeoff. Some of the planes were armed with 11.75-inch "Tiny Tim" rockets, relatively new weapons designed to hit surface targets. *Franklin* was the only carrier in the group with the rockets aboard.

"Early on the morning of 19 March, our aircraft were taking off, all the elevators were up, and the flight deck officer was revving them up for takeoff," remembered Jurika. "About five or six aircraft had gotten off when right out of the fairly low thin clouds a Japanese plane like a carrier attack bomber came right down the length of the *Franklin*'s deck."

The lone enemy plane, its exact type unknown, had slipped undetected through the combat air patrol. In seconds, two 551-pound bombs plummeted toward the carrier.

"I saw this out of the corner of my eye," Jurika wrote, "and I saw two bombs drop from the plane and hit just forward of the forward elevator, and within a fraction of a second, of course, an enormous explosion took place down below and the elevator lifted up, cockeyed, and then fell back down across the elevator opening. The planes just behind the elevator were spotted, ready for takeoff, engines going, fully loaded with Tiny Tims, loaded with five-hundred- and thousand-pound bombs; the entire flight deck aft of the island structure was loaded with aircraft ready to takeoff [sic]."

The two bombs penetrated to the hangar deck and exploded, starting fires and cooking off Tiny Tim rockets that slithered across the deck and through the gaping elevator space. Jurika noted, "From what I could see out the side, and that quickly became obscured with smoke, the planes were exploding on deck. Mark XIII torpedoes were going off right on the deck."

Power was lost, and the *Franklin* went dead in the water with a fifteen-degree list to starboard. Careful counter-flooding helped to correct that situation, but fires were out of control, and the carrier billowed smoke. Many crewmen were trapped below decks and incinerated or asphyxiated by the thick, noxious fumes. Others jumped overboard to save themselves from the raging fires.

The cruiser *Santa Fe* came alongside to render aid, and heroic damage-control efforts eventually got the fires under control. It had been close. No *Essex*-class fleet carriers were lost to enemy action during World War II, but the *Franklin* came nearest. Casualties included 724 killed and 265 wounded.

The cruiser *Pittsburgh* took the *Franklin* in tow until boilers were operational and the carrier could power itself. The *Franklin* proceeded to the anchorage at Ulithi in the Caroline Islands for immediate repairs, then to Pearl Harbor and on through the Panama Canal to the Brooklyn Navy Yard. Following a twelve-thousand-mile odyssey, the burned-out carrier arrived in New York on April 28, forty days after the devastating attack.

The British Royal Navy returned to action in the Pacific Theater in the spring of 1944, participating with the US Navy in joint air attacks against the Japanese-occupied Dutch East Indies. In November the British Pacific Fleet was formed, and eventually the Royal Navy's commitment in the Pacific grew to six fleet carriers, four light carriers, nine escort carriers, and two maintenance carriers that were used to repair aircraft. In addition to American aircraft types, the British carriers transported the Fairey Barracuda torpedo bomber, the Supermarine Seafire (a variant of the famed Spitfire fighter adapted to carrier operations), and amphibious reconnaissance planes.

A US Navy officer aboard an aircraft carrier writes a personal message in memory of a lost comrade. His tablet is the surface of a bomb that will soon be loaded aboard a navy plane going into action against the Japanese. The overwhelming might of American carrier air power eventually crushed the Imperial Japanese Navy in the Pacific while also providing air support for land operations across miles of trackless ocean. *National Archives*

The British fleet carriers included the thirty-six-thousand-ton HMS *Implacable*, *Illustrious*, *Formidable*, *Indefatigable*, *Indomitable*, and *Victorious*, veterans of European Theater operations in the Mediterranean, off the coast of Norway, the attack on the Italian anchorage at Taranto, and the *Bismarck* chase. These carriers launched air strikes against targets in the Japanese home islands and withstood repeated kamikaze attacks. Their armored flight decks offered significant protection against the suicide planes.

LAUNCHED!

The finest light-weight felt hats in the world...100% American hats...made by American workmen

...at American wages...now national best sellers!

STETSON  "VITA-FELTS"

TEN DOLLARS

OTHER STETSONS FROM FIVE DOLLARS

STETSON HATS ARE ALSO MADE IN CANADA

On May 11, 1945, the *Essex*-class aircraft carrier USS *Bunker Hill* was struck by two kamikazes off the coast of Okinawa and became an inferno. One of the Japanese suicide planes had crashed into thirty-four armed and fueled aircraft on the *Bunker Hill*'s flight deck. Three hundred seventy-three American sailors and naval aviators were killed that morning; however, the fires were brought under control and the carrier survived. *National Archives*

The US Navy liaison officer aboard the *Indefatigable* observed, "When a kamikaze hits a US carrier it means six months of repair at Pearl. When a kamikaze hits a Limey carrier, it's just a case of 'Sweepers, man your brooms.'"

The light carriers were those of the thirteen-thousand-ton *Colossus* class, including the HMS *Colossus*, *Glory*, *Vengeance*, and *Venerable*. Sixteen *Colossus*-class light carriers were ordered by the Admiralty in 1942 during the Royal Navy's period of greatest need for aircraft carriers. Four were completed during World War II with complements of forty-eight aircraft each, but none of them saw combat. Their commissions had come at a time when the need for carriers had waned in the European Theater, and they did not reach the Pacific until early 1945.

The *Colossus*-class ships resembled scaled-down versions of the *Illustrious*-class fleet carriers. Four were completed after the war, and although they were considered "disposable" ships intended to serve only about two years, their service lives extended well beyond the threshold. The Admiralty eventually sold surplus *Colossus*-class carriers to seven other navies.

With the surrender of Japan on September 2, 1945, World War II in the Pacific ended. The aircraft carrier had become the weapon of decision in naval warfare and ascended to preeminence among capital ships. Although its use in combat has been limited since 1945, the carrier has remained dominant on the world's naval stage for more than seventy years later.

THE CARRIER IN WAR AND PEACE

The architects of the world's great navies debated the merits of armored flight decks well before the beginning of World War II.

The British Royal Navy opted for better defensive capabilities (i.e., armored flight decks), anticipating the majority of its wartime action to be in the relative confines of the North Sea, the Mediterranean, and areas near the coast of the European continent where its capital ships might be susceptible to attacks from land-based aircraft. In contrast, the US Navy stressed offensive capabilities in light of the need to defend American interests across two vast oceans. Unarmored flight decks allowed larger contingents of aircraft aboard the US carriers.

The Korean War provided a good view of the transition into the jet age aboard aircraft carriers. Here, the pilot of a Grumman F9F Panther fighter climbs into the cockpit of his aircraft as he prepares to follow prop-driven Douglas AD Skyraider and Grumman F4U Corsair attack planes from the flight deck of the *Essex*-class aircraft carrier USS *Princeton*. This photo was taken on May 1, 1951. *National Archives*

The issue with armored flight decks was the simple fact that they weighed more than wooden decks. Placing greater weight at the higher flight deck level contributed to greater potential instability during carrier operations on the open sea. The first option to reduce weight was to decrease the number of aircraft carried aboard the ship. While American carriers were capable of eventually transporting offensive air groups comprising ninety or more planes, the British carriers were often restricted to a significantly reduced number.

During post–World War II analysis, for the first time the world's navies had actual combat performance to evaluate. The merits of the armored flight deck were obvious based on the relative experiences of US and British carriers damaged in attacks by conventional Japanese bombs and kamikaze suicide planes that struck off the coast of Okinawa and elsewhere.

As early as 1940, the US Navy began moving toward the practical application of armored flight decks with its largest World War II–era warships. With an original displacement of

Above: During a special replenishment exercise in February 1958, the USS *Midway* takes on fuel from the USS *Chara*, an *Andromeda*-class attack cargo ship. The *Midway* was launched in March 1945, and commissioned eight days after the surrender of Japan ended World War II that September. In this view, the angled flight deck is prominent, and the forward elevator is lowered. *National Archives*

Opposite: The USS *Franklin D. Roosevelt*, the second of three *Midway*-class aircraft carriers of the US Navy, lies ready for launching ceremonies at the New York Navy Yard on April 29, 1945. The *Midway*-class carriers displaced forty-five thousand tons and were the first carriers of the navy to be constructed with armored flight decks. *National Archives*

The USS *Coral Sea* is shown underway in January 1948. Commissioned in 1947, the *Midway*-class *Coral Sea* was active with the US Navy until the spring of 1990. The *Coral Sea* took part in operations during the Vietnam War, the *Mayaguez* Incident, and unrest in the Middle East. *National Archives*

A Lockheed S3A twin-engine turbojet antisubmarine aircraft sits on the flight deck of the USS *Midway* with its wings folded as deck crewmen begin servicing the plane. The *Midway*-class aircraft carriers were half again as large as their *Essex*-class predecessors and carried up to 140 aircraft. The *Midway* was a long-serving carrier with the navy and is now moored in the harbor of San Diego, California, as a floating museum. *US DefenseImagery, DN-SN-85-06353*

forty-five thousand tons, the future *Midway*-class carriers—the first US aircraft carriers with armored flight decks—would be more than half again as heavy in tonnage as those of the *Essex* class. Through sheer size their aircraft capacity was increased substantially to nearly 140, while the basic hangar and flight deck designs continued: two steam catapults, a pair of centerline elevators, and a third elevator along the deck edge to facilitate aircraft handling.

The *Midway*-class carriers, initially designated as large carriers (CVB), were constructed with a beam of 121 feet, too wide for the 110-foot locks of the Panama Canal, and an overall length of more than one thousand feet. Three carriers—the *Midway*, *Franklin D, Roosevelt*, and *Coral Sea*—were constructed at Newport News Shipbuilding in Virginia and at the Brooklyn Navy Yard, while another three of the class were canceled. The *Midway* was laid down in October 1943, launched in March 1945, and commissioned on September 10 of that year, eight days after the Japanese surrender in Tokyo Bay. The *Franklin D. Roosevelt* was commissioned in October 1945 and became the first US Navy carrier to deploy with

A Ling-Temco-Vought A7E Corsair II aircraft of attack squadron VA-25 approaches the *Forrestal*-class aircraft carrier USS *Ranger* for recovery as other A7E aircraft are made ready for flight operations off the coast of Vietnam. The versatile Corsair entered service with the US Navy in 1967 and was retired in the early 1990s. *National Archives*

THE CARRIER AIR WING

The modern carrier air wing of the US Navy provides the striking power that has defined the role of the aircraft carrier since its inception.

The first carrier air groups of the navy were formed in 1937, and by the early months of World War II the typical air group consisted of a fighter squadron of eighteen Grumman F4F Wildcat fighters, a torpedo squadron of eighteen Douglas TBD Devastator torpedo bombers, a scouting squadron of eighteen Douglas SBD Dauntless dive-bombers, and a bombing squadron of eighteen Dauntlesses. Later in the war, the scouting squadrons were discontinued and new types of aircraft, including the Vought F4U Corsair and Grumman F6F Hellcat fighters, the Curtiss SB2C Helldiver dive-bomber, and the Grumman TBF Avenger torpedo bomber, were included in the standard complement of seventy-two aircraft aboard *Essex*-class carriers.

During the Korean War, the Grumman F9F Panther and the McDonnell F2H Banshee became the first carrier-based jet aircraft to see combat. The carrier air group included two or three squadrons of Panther or Banshee fighter bombers accompanied by up to two squadrons of F4U Corsairs and an attack squadron of Douglas AD Skyraiders.

In December 1963, the carrier air groups were officially redesignated as carrier air wings. By the height of the Vietnam War in the late 1960s, a sophisticated division of labor had emerged. The air wing usually included two fighter squadrons of McDonnell Douglas F-4 Phantoms or Vought F-8 Crusaders, two attack squadrons of Ling-Temco-Vought A-7 Corsairs or Douglas A-4 Skyhawks, an all-weather attack squadron of Grumman A-6 Intruders, and support squadrons for airborne early warning, electronic warfare, and reconnaissance, along with detachments of multipurpose helicopters.

Aircraft types such as the Grumman F-14 Tomcat fighter and the McDonnell Douglas F/A-18 Hornet were deployed during the 1970s, and a full carrier air wing included as many as eleven squadrons of varied aircraft. The F-14 served aboard the navy's carriers for thirty-two years, from 1974 until its retirement in 2006.

Today, the modern US Navy carrier air wing typically includes four strike fighter squadrons of the F/A-18 Hornet or the upgraded Boeing F/A-18 Super Hornet, an electronic warfare squadron of either four Northrop Grumman EA6-B Prowlers or five Boeing EA-18G Growlers, an airborne early-warning squadron of four Northrop Grumman E-2C Hawkeyes, two helicopter combat and strike squadrons of Sikorsky MH-60 helicopters, and a logistics support detachment of two Grumman C-2 Greyhound cargo aircraft.

The bow of the *Essex*-class aircraft carrier USS *Antietam* lies in dry dock in 1952 during the addition of a sponson that made the ship the first angled flight deck carrier in the world. Launched in August 1944 and commissioned the following January, the *Antietam* was one of numerous *Essex*-class aircraft carriers that underwent renovations and remained in service with the US Navy for two decades or more. The *Antietam* was decommissioned in 1963 and sold for scrap in 1974. *National Naval Aviation Museum/Robert L. Lawson Photograph Collection/1996.488.061.039*

nuclear bombs aboard. The *Coral Sea* was commissioned in 1947 and served until the spring of 1990.

As the *Midway*-class carriers entered service, the role of the carrier as a capital ship continued to evolve. At the dawn of the nuclear age, and with the Cold War ascendant, a rivalry developed between the US Navy, with its carriers, and the US Air Force, with its long-range strategic bombers. The interservice argument over the primary method of delivery of nuclear weapons had far-reaching consequences related to American military doctrine, budgetary concerns, and geopolitical issues.

Nevertheless, the *Midway*-class carriers served for decades. The lead ship of the class, the USS *Midway*, was

decommissioned in 1992 after a remarkable forty-seven-year career. The *Midway* was the first ship of its kind to be forward-deployed, based at Yokosuka, Japan, for seventeen years, and more than two hundred thousand US Navy personnel served aboard the carrier through half a century and operations from the Mediterranean to Vietnam to Desert Storm. The *Midway* carriers underwent significant modernization during the mid-1950s with the addition of angled flight decks to facilitate jet aircraft operations, improved steam catapults, stronger flight decks and elevators, and enclosed hurricane bows that protected forward areas from the elements.

Due to high costs, the USS *Midway* was the lone ship of the class to undergo another round of modernization a decade later, and in 1986 an effort to improve buoyancy by adding bulges to the hull actually had the opposite effect, causing the ship to roll more heavily. By the end of its career, the *Midway*'s air wing had been reduced to approximately fifty-five planes due to the increased size and weight of modern aircraft in comparison to the World War II–era piston-engine planes she had been originally designed to carry. The carrier could not accommodate large aircraft such as the Grumman F-14 Tomcat fighter or the Lockheed S-3 Viking antisubmarine aircraft; however, on its final deployment the carrier's air wing included four squadrons of McDonnell Douglas F/A-18 Hornet multi-role combat aircraft and two squadrons of Grumman A-6 Intruder strike aircraft. Today, the *Midway* is moored at San Diego's Navy Pier as a floating museum open to the public.

During the postwar years, the *Essex*-class carriers continued to serve as the workhorses of the US Navy's seaborne strike capability. A number of the carriers underwent significant modernization with some altered to serve as antisubmarine (CVS) carriers or other specialized types; however, by the early 1970s purpose-built carriers were being considered for these tasks.

The USS *Oriskany* was the last of the *Essex*-class carriers completed. She was laid down at the Brooklyn Navy Yard on May 1, 1944, and commissioned on September 25, 1950. Construction of the *Oriskany* was halted in 1946 when the carrier was roughly 85 percent complete and resumed the following year with modifications to her original design under the extensive SCB-27 modernization program. Under this program, the *Oriskany* served as the prototype for another fourteen *Essex*-class carriers completed between 1950 and 1955. Subsequently, several of these ships were redesignated as attack carriers (from CV to CVA).

SCB-27 included relocation and redesign of the carrier island, reinforcement of the flight deck to accommodate heavier and faster jet aircraft, rearrangement or removal of certain antiaircraft weapons, larger elevators, and the standardization of all carriers with clipper bows, eliminating the short hull and long hull (sometimes referred to as the *Ticonderoga* class) distinctions among *Essex*-class carriers.

Although a port sponson was fitted to the flight deck of the USS *Antietam* in 1952, in effect making the carrier the world's first with an angled flight deck, another modernization program, designated SCB-125, reconfigured fourteen *Essex*-class carriers with the angled flight decks between 1954 and 1959. These angled decks have since become hallmarks of jet fighter operations in the twentieth century. Additional SCB-125 improvements included enclosed hurricane bows, air conditioning, improved arresting gear, lengthened or relocated

elevators, and the relocation of primary flight control to the aft end of the carrier island. Five of the modified *Essex*-class carriers—the *Hornet*, *Lexington*, *Bennington*, *Bon Homme Richard*, and *Oriskany*—are sometimes referred to as the *Hancock* class.

The antisubmarine conversions began in the late 1950s and included the *Hornet*, *Lexington*, and *Bennington*, which were equipped with submarine-tracking aircraft and fighters to provide air cover. This *Essex*-class USS *Lexington*, the last of the class to be decommissioned, ended its career in 1991. During its lengthy service (it was commissioned in 1943), the *Lexington* functioned as a standard carrier, attack carrier, antisubmarine warfare carrier, and training carrier.

The aforementioned controversy related to preeminence among the US armed forces in the nuclear age led to a bitterly divisive episode that ended the construction of the US Navy's first planned "supercarrier" and, according to some historians, actually threatened the survival of the aircraft carrier as a weapon of war. The Naval Appropriations Act of 1949 authorized funding for the construction of five aircraft carriers, each displacing sixty-five thousand tons and commanding a price tag of at least $190 million. The previous summer President Harry Truman had approved the building program, and the keel of the first supercarrier, the USS *United States*, was laid at Newport News Shipbuilding on April 18, 1949.

The design of the *United States* was a radical departure from those of previous carriers. The massive warship was to be flush-decked, without an island superstructure, and designed to handle modern jet aircraft that weighed at least half a ton and were capable of carrying nuclear bombs. At 1,090 feet long, the carrier was to be powered by boilers and steam turbines generating 280,000 shaft horsepower with a top speed of thirty-three knots. Its aircraft complement would include forty-five McDonnell F2H Banshee fighters and the strike capability of a dozen Douglas A-3 Skywarrior bombers. The crew would total more than three thousand sailors and airmen.

Giving in to pressure from the Joint Chiefs of Staff, particularly the senior commanders of the US Air Force and the US Army, Secretary of Defense Louis Johnson canceled the construction of the *United States* just five days after its keel was laid. The Air Force contingent argued that the *United States* was prohibitively expensive during an era of postwar austerity and that its long-distance nuclear strike capability was redundant considering the Air Force heavy bombers had been designed to carry nuclear weapons. With the cancellation announcement, Secretary of the Navy John Sullivan abruptly resigned.

During the critical months that followed, the defense budget for fiscal 1951 was debated. Serious cuts in naval spending were proposed, including the reduction of operational *Essex*-class carriers by 50 percent to four; the reduction of carrier air groups from fourteen to six and marine

In frigid waters off the coast of Korea, crewmen sweep snow from the flight deck of the *Essex*-class aircraft carrier USS *Valley Forge* on December 26, 1951. Grumman F9F Panther fighters, one of the earliest carrier-based jet aircraft types deployed with the US Navy, sit with their wings folded and await cleaning as well. The first US air strikes of the Korean War were launched from the deck of the *Valley Forge* and the British Royal Navy light carrier HMS *Triumph*. *National Archives*

A Douglas AD-4 Skyraider crashes on the deck of the *Essex*-class aircraft carrier USS *Philippine Sea* on return from a hazardous mission in the skies above North Korea. The Skyraider was a prop-driven attack aircraft that first deployed with carrier-based navy squadrons in the late 1940s. More than three thousand were eventually built, and the Skyraider's lengthy service life extended through the Vietnam War and into the 1980s. *US DefenseImagery, 80-G-423867*

air squadrons from twenty-three to twelve; a pronounced reduction of antisubmarine capability; and more. At the same time, the Air Force proposed an increase of strategic bombing forces to at least seventy bomb groups.

The subsequent "Revolt of the Admirals" was marked by vocal dissatisfaction with the changes in priorities. Chief of Naval Operations Admiral Louis Denfeld was forced to resign as a result, while other naval officers paid a severe price for their objections. However, naval aviation and the future of the aircraft carrier were saved due in large part to their dissent and to the outbreak of the Korean War.

The US Navy initially shouldered a significant burden in the response to the North Korean invasion of South Korea on June 25, 1950, and the value of the aircraft carrier in rapid response to global hotspots became readily apparent. Senior Navy commanders were assured that funding for a supercarrier would come in the near future.

Meanwhile, following a United Nations resolution authorizing action against the North Korean aggressor, the US armed forces led a broad coalition under the UN banner, including significant naval assets. Because their operations included support of ground troops, aerial combat against enemy planes, and tactical and strategic air strikes against military, logistics, and transportation targets, aircraft carriers of the US and British Royal navies appeared to be in violation of three basic tenets of carrier warfare: avoid direct decisive engagements with land forces unless the carrier force is decidedly superior in strength; do not tether a mobile carrier force to a limited area of land; and maintain a concentrated strength posture.

However, the virtual absence of enemy naval assets, the defensive capabilities of the carriers and their escorts against air or seaborne attack, and the demands of the land war itself mitigated the risks involved and justified the actions just as they would in the role carriers played during the Vietnam War more than a decade later.

The first UN air strikes of the Korean War were launched from the deck of the carrier USS *Valley Forge* and the Royal

continued on page 167

A Grumman F9F Panther jet fighter is raised on an elevator to the flight deck of a US Navy aircraft carrier during operations off the east coast of Korea in mid-July 1950. The aircraft carriers of the US Navy and British Royal Navy supplied much of the air support for ground troops battling the communist aggressors that invaded South Korea in the summer of 1950. This photo was taken days after the war began. *National Archives*

Above: A Grumman F9F-3 Panther taxis forward on USS *Valley Forge* to be catapulted for strikes on targets along the east coast of Korea in July 1950. Note details of the ship's island, including the chalk scoreboard just visible at lower left. *Naval History and Heritage Command/80-G-428152*

Opposite: Grumman F4U Corsair fighters take off from the deck of a US Navy aircraft carrier in June 1950, while busy crewmen perform their assigned tasks and the next F4U in line, armed with rockets, awaits the signal to take off. A World War II vintage fighter, the Corsair found new life during the Korean Conflict as an attack aircraft, providing support to ground troops with machine gun and rocket fire. *National Archives*

continued from page 163

Navy *Colossus*-class light carrier HMS *Triumph* on July 3, 1950. At the time, the *Valley Forge* was the sole American carrier operating in the Western Pacific, while the *Triumph* was sailing in the Yellow Sea. Pilots of US Navy Carrier Air Group Five flew Grumman F9F Panther fighters and Douglas AD Skyraider attack aircraft in the first combat action for either type. Royal Navy airmen flew the propeller-driven Fairey Firefly FR and Supermarine Seafire fighters.

One of the most spectacular carrier-based air missions of the Korean War involved a Skyraider strike against the Hwachon Dam in South Korea. On the morning of May 1, 1951, five Skyraiders of squadron VA-195 and three from squadron VC-35, escorted by eight Vought F4U Corsair fighters of squadrons VF-192 and VF-193, flew from the deck of the carrier USS *Princeton*. The Skyraiders were armed with Mark 13 torpedoes, unusual ordnance for an attack against a

Above: Spray breaks over the bow of the *Essex*-class aircraft carrier USS *Leyte* and douses Grumman F9F Panther fighters parked on the flight deck as the ship crosses the International Date Line en route to Korean waters in September 1950. In 1953, work began to convert the *Leyte* to an antisubmarine carrier. *National Archives*

Opposite: Grumman F4U Corsair attack planes sit on the flight deck of a US Navy aircraft carrier off the coast of Korea. Crewmen busily arm some of these aircraft for an upcoming mission in support of United Nations troops operating on the Korean peninsula. Those Corsairs already armed, their missiles visible on folded wings, await the start of the mission. *Naval History and Heritage Command/NH 97059*

Left: Lieutenant J. W. Fornof inspects damage to the wing of his Grumman F9F Panther fighter after returning safely from a mission over Korea to the *Essex*-class aircraft carrier USS *Boxer*. The *Boxer* was launched in December 1944 and was later redesigned as an amphibious assault ship. *National Archives*

Below: In this photo taken in April 1951 aboard the *Independence*-class light aircraft carrier USS *Bataan*, US Navy pilots have just returned from a mission against enemy positions on the Korean peninsula and discuss its results. Some carrier pilots who served during the Korean War were veterans of World War II, while others were reservists called to active duty. *National Archives*

land target, but the results were dramatic: six of them found their mark and destroyed the dam.

At any given time during the Korean War, up to four US fleet aircraft carriers operated off the Korean peninsula. While no *Midway*-class carriers were deployed to the Pacific during the conflict, the *Essex*-class carriers were heavily involved. During the desperate fighting at the Chosin Reservoir in the winter of 1950, planes from the *Valley Forge*, *Philippine Sea*, *Princeton*, and *Leyte* provided critical close air support to ground troops. Among the Royal Navy carriers active during the Korean War, the *Colossus*-class carrier HMS *Glory* deployed three times, while her sister the HMS *Theseus* launched 3,500 aircraft sorties during a seven-month span from September 1950 to April 1951.

Royal Navy aircraft carrier construction begun during World War II continued into the postwar years and included

F4U-4 Corsairs of the US Marine Corps' all-weather "Polka Dot" squadron (a.k.a. the "Moonlighters") await ordnance on the last day of the Korean War. Assigned ground targets, the squadron racked up an impressive record of destruction in their short time in Korea. The squadron flew its last flight in 2007. *Department of Defense photo*

continued on page 177

Two Grumman F9F Panther fighters streak past the *Essex*-class aircraft carrier USS *Princeton* on May 23, 1951. The Panthers often flew escort duty for Grumman Corsairs and Douglas Skyraiders conducting operations against the Korean infrastructure, such as those that flew from the *Princeton* on the mission against the Hwachon Dam on May 1, 1951. *National Archives*

U.S.S. PRINCETON

CVS - 37

Above: The British Royal Navy aircraft carrier HMS *Eagle* steams in the open sea as a helicopter comes alongside in preparation for landing. Launched in March 1946, the *Eagle* was the first of two carriers of the World War II–era *Audacious* class to be completed and was deployed during the Suez Crisis of the mid-1950s. The second *Audacious*-class carrier completed was the *Ark Royal*, commissioned in 1955. These carriers displaced 36,800 tons and carried fifty aircraft. *Royal Navy photo*

Opposite: Developed from the highly successful land-based Hawker Tempest fighter bomber, a Hawker Sea Fury, the last propeller-driven aircraft to serve aboard the aircraft carriers of the British Royal Navy, clears the flight deck of the carrier HMS *Glory* in June 1951. The *Glory* deployed three times during the Korean War and was eventually sold for scrap in 1961. *National Archives*

Planes and helicopters sit on the flight deck of the *Colossus*-class aircraft carrier HMS *Glory* of the British Royal Navy in July 1951. The *Colossus*-class carriers displaced 13,400 tons and carried up to forty-eight aircraft. This photograph was taken from aboard the escort carrier USS *Sicily*. *National Archives*

In August 1967, approximately a month after a devastating fire touched off by a faulty mechanism that inadvertently launched a rocket aboard the ship and killed 134 sailors, the USS *Forrestal* conducts flight operations in the Gulf of Tonkin off the coast of Vietnam. Commissioned on October 1, 1955, the *Forrestal* was the lead ship of the class that is considered the first of the US Navy's supercarriers, displacing more than sixty thousand tons. *US Navy photo/PHC H. L. Wise, USN*

The *Forrestal*-class aircraft carrier USS *Ranger* steams off the coast of Vietnam in 1966. The *Forrestal*-class carriers incorporated a number of the improvements that were envisioned with the USS *United States*, a supercarrier that was canceled after its keel was laid. The controversy that followed sparked the "Revolt of the Admirals" in the early 1950s. The *Ranger* was commissioned on August 10, 1957. *National Naval Aviation Museum/2001.205.081*

continued from page 169

the *Colossus*-class light carriers and the similar designs of the *Majestic* class. The six *Majestic*-class carriers were modified to accommodate larger aircraft as the war progressed, and though their construction was suspended in 1945, a total of five were eventually finished, the last being commissioned in 1961. These carriers—the *Majestic*, *Magnificent*, *Hercules*, *Powerful*, and *Terrible*—were either sold or loaned to the navies of Australia, Canada, and India. In 1948, the *Terrible* entered service with the Royal Australian Navy as HMAS *Sydney*, and during the Korean War the carrier launched a record number of sorties in a single day: eighty-nine on October 11, 1951.

The largest World War II–era Royal Navy fleet carriers were laid down as the *Audacious* class in 1942 and 1943. These were originally intended as an expansion of the *Implacable* class, but concerns related to the height of the hangar deck and its ability to accommodate more modern aircraft resulted in an enlargement. The carriers displaced 36,800 tons with lengths of 804 feet and a top speed of thirty-two knots delivered by eight Admiralty boilers and four sets of Parsons geared turbines producing 152,000 shaft horsepower. They carried up to fifty aircraft.

Originally named HMS *Audacious*, the first of the class was renamed and launched as the HMS *Eagle* in March

1946, by Harland and Wolff of Belfast, Northern Ireland. The second was originally named the HMS *Irresistible* but renamed the *Ark Royal* and launched in 1950 by Cammell Laird of Birkenhead. The last two carriers of the class were canceled. The HMS *Eagle* was deployed during the Suez Crisis of 1956, and its contemporary aircraft complement included the prop-driven Westland Wyvern fighter, the Hawker Sea Hawk jet fighter, the de Havilland Sea Venom jet fighter bomber, and the American-built Douglas AD Skyraider. The *Eagle* underwent major modifications and was eventually decommissioned in 1972. The *Ark Royal* was commissioned in 1955 and ultimately scrapped twenty-five years later after efforts to preserve the carrier as a museum failed.

The last of the Royal Navy's carriers laid down during World War II were the four ships of the *Centaur* class, whose displacement was roughly similar to the *Essex* class's twenty-seven thousand tons. Construction on these carriers began in the spring of 1944; following suspensions of work at the end of the war, each was commissioned during the 1950s. A combination of Admiralty boilers and Parsons geared turbines generated seventy-six thousand shaft horsepower and a top speed of twenty-eight knots. The carriers transported up to forty-two planes.

Although the *Centaur* retained its original flight deck configuration, the other three carriers of the class—the *Albion*, *Bulwark*, and *Hermes*—were fitted with angled flight decks as their design was modified during construction. The *Bulwark* served into the 1980s, and the *Hermes*, best known for its role in the 1982 Falklands War with Argentina, was sold to the Indian navy in 1986, was renamed the INS *Viraat*, and remains in service today.

For more than thirty years after the end of World War II, British carrier construction was discontinued. The four carriers of the *Malta* class, each displacing nearly fifty-eight thousand tons, were canceled at the end of 1945, while the two carriers of the *Queen Elizabeth* class, at more than fifty-five thousand tons, were canceled in 1966.

The US Navy's first operational supercarriers emerged from the turmoil of the interservice rivalry that had spawned the Revolt of the Admirals and the practical experience of the Korean War, which demonstrated the value of a carrier force capable of responding rapidly to a military threat anywhere in the world. The four supercarriers of the *Forrestal* class, named for Secretary of Defense James Forrestal, were laid down from mid-1952 to 1955 at Newport News Shipbuilding and the New York Naval Shipyard. They included the *Forrestal*, *Saratoga*, *Ranger*, and *Independence*, and each displaced approximately sixty thousand tons. These were the first aircraft carriers designed and built from the keel up since the end of World War II. Initially classified as large carriers (CVB), they were redesignated as attack carriers (CVA) in the autumn of 1952.

The *Forrestal* class's original design included straight flight decks and incorporated a number of the innovations that had been planned for the canceled USS *United States*. The *Forrestal* was modified with an angled flight deck while under construction, and the remaining carriers were subsequently built with angled flight decks. Their spacious hangar decks were 740 feet long, 101 feet wide, and 25 feet high. Armored flight decks were incorporated into the hull; the resulting platforms were highly stable with good seakeeping characteristics.

At 1,070 feet, the *Forrestals* were 100 feet longer than the *Midway*-class carriers, and twenty feet wider at the beam at 130 feet. Their boilers and steam turbines produced 280,000 shaft horsepower and a top speed of thirty-four knots. They were conspicuous with their large islands and distinguished by their three elevators, one forward of the island and two aft, with the port elevator located on the forward edge of the flight deck. Their aircraft capacity was up to one hundred planes of various types.

In the 1970s, the *Forrestal*-class carriers were redesignated as multimission carriers (CV) modified to operate air wings that included the S-3 Viking antisubmarine aircraft and SH-3 Sea King antisubmarine helicopter. During the 1980s, the carriers underwent extensive modernization through the Service Life Extension Program (SLEP) initiative, including improved radar and communications equipment, enhanced propulsion systems, and the rehabilitation of the ships' hulls following extensive deployments. Antiaircraft defenses were steadily upgraded, from five-inch guns mounted in sponsons to Sea Sparrow missiles with the Mark 91 Fire Control System. After modernization, the *Ranger* was the only carrier of the class to retain the sponsons.

By the mid-1950s, the *Kitty Hawk*–class carriers, based on a modified *Forrestal* design, were under construction at Newport News and at the Brooklyn Navy Yard and New York Shipbuilding in Camden, New Jersey. The primary improvement in the successor class came about due to practical experience. The *Forrestal* carriers' elevator arrangement impeded flight operations with the portside elevator forward on the angled deck—directly in the launch and landing paths of two of the carriers' catapults. In the *Kitty Hawks* the port elevator was moved to the aft side of the angle, while the locations of the island and second starboard elevator were swapped. Thus, two elevators were forward of the island rather than one as in the *Forrestal* class.

The *Kitty Hawk* was commissioned on April 29, 1961, followed by the *Constellation* that October, the *America* in January 1965, and the *John F. Kennedy* on September 7, 1968. Construction on the *Kitty Hawk* was delayed due to problems at the New Jersey shipyard, and on the *Constellation* due to an onboard fire prior to completion. Notably, the *America* was the

Ordnancemen wearing their distinctive red jerseys aboard the sixty-one-thousand-ton aircraft carrier USS *Constellation* load bombs from carts onto hard points beneath the wings of McDonnell Douglas F-4 Phantom fighter bombers in preparation for a mission against targets in Vietnam. Commissioned in October 1961, the USS *Constellation* was the second of the conventionally powered *Kitty Hawk*-class supercarriers of the US Navy. *National Archives*

only postwar US Navy carrier constructed with a sonar system at the time.

The *John F. Kennedy* was completed after a plan to convert the design from conventional to nuclear power was discarded. The carrier was also built to a modified design and is sometimes considered the single carrier of a distinct class. The revisions included the incorporation of an underwater protection system originally developed for nuclear carriers, a uniquely angled funnel designed to prevent carrier exhaust from obscuring the vision of landing pilots, and a sonar dome (though sonar equipment was never installed). The *Kitty Hawk*, *Constellation*, and *America* were equipped with Terrier

antiaircraft missiles, while the *John F. Kennedy* mounted Sea Sparrow systems. The first three carriers were 1,069 feet long and displaced nearly sixty-one thousand tons; the *John F. Kennedy* was seventeen feet shorter and slightly heavier.

From 1987 to 1992, the *Kitty Hawk* and *Constellation* underwent SLEP modernization intended to add fifteen years to their service lives at the cost of $785 million and $800 million, respectively. The *John F. Kennedy* underwent a separate modernization at a cost of nearly $500 million. When the *Independence* was decommissioned in 1998, the *Kitty Hawk* became the longest tenured warship in the modern US Navy, including ten years as the forward-deployment carrier based

Left: The USS *John F. Kennedy* is shown underway in this aerial view with planes parked on its flight deck. The *John F. Kennedy* was seventeen feet shorter and slightly heavier than the standard *Kitty Hawk*-class carriers. *National Naval Aviation Museum/Robert L. Lawson Photograph Collection/1996.488.128.039*

Opposite: The flight deck director gives a hand signal to the pilot of a Douglas A-4 Skyhawk aircraft of attack squadron VA-81 as it readies for takeoff from the USS *John F. Kennedy* in November 1968. Originally conceived as a nuclear-powered carrier, the *John F. Kennedy* was later launched with conventional steam propulsion. Commissioned on September 7, 1968, the carrier was a modified version of the *Kitty Hawk* class. *National Archives*

at Yokosuka, Japan. When this deployment was completed in 2008, the *Kitty Hawk* sailed to Bremerton, Washington, and was decommissioned the following spring. The *America* was decommissioned in 1996, the *Constellation* in 2003, and the *John F. Kennedy* in 2007.

In the midst of the *Kitty Hawk* construction program, the keel of the US Navy's first nuclear-powered aircraft carrier (CVN), the USS *Enterprise*, was laid at Newport News on February 4, 1958. The historic warship was launched on September 24, 1960, and commissioned on November 25, 1961. With an estimated construction cost of $444 million, the *Enterprise* was completed on a modified *Kitty Hawk* design with a distinctive island structure required to accommodate billboard radar antennae.

At 1,123 feet, the *Enterprise* remains the world's longest naval vessel. Displacing 75,700 standard tons, the carrier was estimated at the time of construction to have a cruising range

Above: Numerous aircraft types, including the McDonnell Douglas F-4 Phantom, the Douglas A-4 Skyraider, the Northrop Grumman EA-6B Prowler, and others sit parked on the flight deck of the *Kitty Hawk*–class aircraft carrier USS *Constellation* in 1967. The dark aircraft at center is a Douglas A-3 Skywarrior strategic bomber, one of the longest serving aircraft in navy history. The Skywarrior entered service in 1956 and was retired in 1991. The *Constellation* was sold for scrap after a forty-two-year career with the US Navy that ended in 2003. *National Naval Aviation Museum/1996.253.3812*

Opposite: McDonnell Douglas F-4 Phantom fighter bombers sit on the hangar deck of the nuclear-powered aircraft carrier USS *Enterprise* in the South China Sea in April 1966. From 1965 to 1975, the *Enterprise* made six deployments to the South China Sea in support operations during the Vietnam War and in response to the North Korean seizure of the intelligence ship USS *Pueblo* in early 1968. *National Archives*

of more than two hundred thousand nautical miles without refueling its eight Westinghouse A2W nuclear reactors. The reactors powered four sets of steam turbines generating 280,000 shaft horsepower and a top speed of more than thirty-three knots. Its aircraft complement totaled up to ninety planes.

Although the *Enterprise* was intended as the first of six ships, she remains literally in a class by herself. Due to excessive cost, the carrier was not equipped with Terrier antiaircraft missiles as planned, and no guns were installed. In 1967, a pair of Sea Sparrow Mark 25 missile launchers were installed, and later upgrades included improved Sea Sparrows and the Phalanx CIWS (Close-in Weapons System). The carrier underwent a three-year modernization and overhaul at the Puget Sound Navy Shipyard from 1979 to 1982, one of two dozen maintenance and refueling programs completed during its long career, with the most recent occurring from 2008 to 2010.

From August to October 1964, the *Enterprise*, the guided missile cruiser USS *Long Beach*, and the frigate USS *Bainbridge* formed Task Force 1, the world's first nuclear naval task force, sailing around the world in sixty-four days and covering 32,600 nautical miles without refueling or reprovisioning. The following year, the carrier became the first nuclear-powered warship of its type to enter combat, when she began flight operations during the Vietnam War. From 1965 to 1975, the *Enterprise* made six deployments to the Western Pacific, either during the Vietnam War or with Task Force 71 (which also included the carriers *Ticonderoga*, *Ranger*, and *Hornet*), deployed in response to the North Korean seizure of the intelligence ship USS *Pueblo* in January 1968.

In 2012, the *Enterprise* was deactivated following a career that spanned more than half a century, including deployments during unrest in the Middle East, the Mediterranean, the Persian Gulf, and Operation Iraqi Freedom. Removal of the carrier's nuclear reactors should be completed by 2017, to be followed by a formal decommissioning ceremony.

Throughout nearly fifteen years of US military involvement in Southeast Asia, the navy carrier force was an active participant. A surge of communist aggression in Laos, Cambodia, and Vietnam at various times prompted the deployment of carrier groups to the region as early as 1959. The carriers of the *Essex*, *Midway*, *Forrestal*, and *Kitty Hawk* classes, along with the *Enterprise*, participated in air strikes, surveillance, and support missions. In the spring of 1961, the bulk of the Seventh Fleet deployed off the coast of Vietnam for possible action in Laos. Two carrier groups were led by the *Coral Sea* and *Midway*, along with the *Kearsarge*, reconfigured

A US Navy pilot places his hand on an air-to-air missile that arms his plane on the deck of the USS *Enterprise*. The *Enterprise* served with the US Navy for more than fifty years, including deployments from the Vietnam era to Operation Iraqi Freedom. *National Naval Aviation Museum/1996.488.022.030*

A Douglas A-4 Skyhawk aircraft of attack squadron VA-34 is directed toward its launching position on the flight deck of the USS *Saratoga* during operations off the coast of Vietnam in 1966. Nearly three thousand Skyhawks were produced from 1954 to 1979, and the last were retired from the US Navy in 2003. The *Forrestal*-class *Saratoga* was commissioned in April 1956 and served with the navy for thirty-six years. *National Naval Aviation Museum/1996.253.4699*

as an antisubmarine carrier, and a helicopter carrier. A year later, the *Hancock* carrier group and the *Bennington*, leading a submarine hunter-killer group, were in the South China Sea.

Following the Gulf of Tonkin Incident in 1964, sixteen bombers from the *Ticonderoga* hit oil-storage facilities in North Vietnam and patrol vessels off the coast, while Douglas Skyraiders and A-4 Skyhawks from Carrier Air Wing 14 aboard the *Constellation* struck naval craft in coastal areas. On February 11, 1965, a total of ninety-five planes from the *Ranger*, *Coral Sea*, and *Hancock* bombed North Vietnamese installations at Qui Nhon during Operation Flaming Dart II.

For extended periods beginning in the spring of 1964, a geographic point that came to be known as Yankee Station served as the locus of flight operations for Task Force 77 as twenty-one of the navy's twenty-three operational carriers

completed at least one Vietnam War–era cruise. Typically three carriers were operational for a twelve-hour period and then rotated with another three, providing twenty-four-hour air capability. The *Kitty Hawk* was the first carrier to take up position at Yankee Station, and on at least one occasion six carriers were operating "on the line" at the same time. From May 1965 until August 1966, when enough land-based aircraft were available to provide support, a single navy carrier operated in the South China Sea at Dixie Station near the Mekong Delta.

Striking North Vietnamese and Viet Cong shipping, bridges, infrastructure, and troop concentrations while also engaging enemy Soviet-made MiG fighters in air-to-air combat, navy pilots flew countless sorties in North Vietnamese airspace. On December 15, 1966, for example,

Above: A McDonnell Douglas F-4 Phantom fighter bomber prepares for takeoff from the deck of the *Forrestal*-class aircraft carrier USS *Saratoga* in 1967. The air campaign against North Vietnam was prosecuted around the clock from a geographic point known as Yankee Station in the Gulf of Tonkin, and during the Vietnam War thousands of carrier-based sorties were flown against military targets and the civilian infrastructure of North Vietnam. *National Naval Aviation Museum/Robert L. Lawson Photograph Collection/1996.253.7278.002*

Above right: A Northrop Grumman EA-6B Prowler all-weather attack aircraft sits with folded wings aboard the nuclear aircraft carrier USS *Nimitz*. Launched in 1975, the *Nimitz* was the second of the US Navy's nuclear-powered aircraft carriers and the lead ship of a class that has been in service with modifications for more than forty years. *National Naval Aviation Museum/ De Angelo, PHAN C.J. USN/1996.253.7059.001*

the *Enterprise* sailed from the Philippine island of Leyte for Yankee Station in company with the destroyer *Manley*, the guided missile cruiser *Gridley*, and the frigate *Bainbridge*. The carrier reached the line at Yankee Station three days later, and air operations commenced immediately. When the carrier left the line on June 20, 1967, *Enterprise* pilots had flown 13,400 missions during 132 days of combat operations. The skies above the communist capital of Hanoi and the port city of Haiphong were the most hazardous on Earth, with defensive SA-2 surface-to-air missiles and a variety of Soviet- and Chinese-supplied antiaircraft guns ringing potential targets around the cities. The carriers were active during the

interdiction and strategic and tactical bombing campaigns codenamed Operation Rolling Thunder, Linebacker, and Linebacker II.

A decade after the US Navy ordered the *Enterprise*, as US involvement in the Vietnam War escalated, its second nuclear aircraft carrier, the USS *Nimitz*, was authorized. Today the *Nimitz* class includes ten carriers, the largest warships in active service in the world. The lead ship of the class was laid down on June 22, 1968, launched in the spring of 1972, and commissioned on May 3, 1975. The most recent *Nimitz*-class addition to the fleet is the USS *George H. W. Bush*, commissioned on January 10, 2009.

Following a course of construction spanning thirty-five years, the *Nimitz*-class carriers may be grouped into three subclasses: the original *Nimitz*, the *Theodore Roosevelt*, and the *Ronald Reagan*. Slightly different designs are apparent, and the *Ronald Reagan* subclass is intended as a transitional move to the new *Gerald R. Ford* class scheduled for commissioning in 2016.

The *Nimitz*-class carriers are 1,092 feet long and 134 feet wide at the beam, and they displace more than seventy thousand tons light. With full complements of personnel, aircraft, and provisions, the carriers displace nearly one hundred thousand tons. Their two Westinghouse A4W nuclear reactors power four steam turbines and produce 260,000 shaft horsepower with a top speed of more than thirty knots. The *Nimitz* and *Dwight D. Eisenhower* were ordered initially as attack carriers (CVAN) and later changed to the CVN designation. Other carriers in the class include the *Carl Vinson*, *Abraham Lincoln*, *George Washington*, *John C. Stennis*, and *Harry S. Truman*. Aircraft embarked aboard these carriers include up to ninety planes and helicopters.

In this 1980 photo, crewmen perform maintenance on an RH-53 Sea Stallion helicopter on the hangar deck of the nuclear aircraft carrier USS *Nimitz*. With a length of 1,092 feet and a displacement of approximately one hundred thousand tons fully loaded, the *Nimitz*-class carriers are the largest warships in active service in the world today. The CH-53 heavy lift cargo transport helicopter was retired from navy service in 2012 but remains active with other forces around the globe. *Department of Defense photo*

Left: Crewmen roll missiles on a cart to the wings of a waiting Grumman F-14 Tomcat fighter aboard the *Forrestal*-class aircraft carrier USS *Saratoga* in the Gulf of Sidra. During the period that this photo was taken, F-14s engaged Libyan targets in one of three incidents that occurred off the coast of Libya in the 1980s as the US Navy enforced the right of free passage through disputed waters. *The LIFE Picture Collection/Getty Images*

Opposite: Several aircraft from Carrier Air Wing 3 (CVW-3) sit on the flight deck of the aircraft carrier USS *John F. Kennedy*. The carrier plows through stormy seas on March 12, 1986, with a variety of its air wing's aircraft visible. They include (front) a Lockheed S-3A Viking (antisubmarine); (fourth from front) a Grumman EA-6B Prowler (electronic countermeasures); and host of Grumman A-6E Intruders. *Department of Defense photo/PH1 Phil Wiggins, US Navy*

Below: A McDonnell Douglas FG1 Phantom jet fighter of the No. 892 Naval Air Squadron sits on the flight deck of the *Audacious*-class aircraft carrier HMS *Ark Royal* in 1972. Commissioned in 1955, the *Ark Royal* served with the British Royal Navy until it was sold for scrap in 1980. *National Naval Aviation Museum/1996.253.7324.004*

During the troubled latter half of the twentieth century, the US government called upon the navy's aircraft carriers regularly to support limited military operations, to ensure free passage through disputed waters, and as instruments of foreign policy and diplomacy. In 1975, the *Saratoga*'s air wing flew covering missions during the Marine Corps' operation to rescue the merchant ship *Mayaguez*, illegally seized by the Cambodian Khmer Rouge. In October 1983, a battle group led by the *Independence* supported land operations on the Caribbean island of Grenada, and later that year the carrier returned to the Eastern Mediterranean and launched air strikes against Syrian military operations threatening the political stability of Lebanon. While escorting Kuwaiti-flagged tankers through the Persian Gulf in 1988 during the so-called Tanker War between Iran and Iraq, the *Enterprise*

launched aircraft that sank one hostile Iranian Navy frigate and damaged another.

In the 1980s when Libyan dictator Muammar Qaddafi declared a "Line of Death" in the waters of the neighboring Gulf of Sidra beyond the recognized twelve-mile territorial limit, the US Navy acted to ensure freedom of navigation. Three separate incidents occurred, the first on August 19, 1981, when Grumman F-14 Tomcat fighters from the carriers *Nimitz* and *Forrestal* responded to aggressive acts by Libyan planes and *Nimitz* pilots shot down two Soviet-made Sukhoi Su-22 fighters.

In March 1986, the carriers *America*, *Coral Sea*, and *Saratoga* again challenged the Libyan claim to the Gulf of Sidra. After the Libyans fired surface-to-air missiles at two Tomcats from the *America*, navy fighters, A-6 and A-7 attack planes, and surface ships responded, sinking a Libyan naval corvette and

Crewmen and naval aviators lounge on the flight deck of the British Royal Navy aircraft carrier HMS *Hermes* during the long voyage to the South Atlantic during the Falklands War of 1982. The air power aboard the *Hermes* and the light carrier *Invincible*, the twenty-two-thousand-ton lead ship of its class, proved decisive during the brief but violent clash with the Argentine armed forces over possession of the Falkland Islands. *Hulton Archive/Getty Images*

a patrol boat and damaging two other vessels. Air attacks also crippled Libyan surface-to-air missile sites. In the third Gulf of Sidra incident, Tomcats from the carrier *John F. Kennedy* shot down two Libyan MiG-23 fighters on January 4, 1989.

In the spring of 1982, the military junta governing Argentina seized the Falkland Islands, which the Argentines had claimed as their own despite the fact that the specks of land in the South Atlantic had long been British territory. The British responded by sending troops to retake the islands along with a naval task force led by the venerable carrier *Hermes*, which had been due for decommissioning, and the new light carrier *Invincible*, the lead ship of a class of three carriers—the other two being the *Illustrious* and *Ark Royal*—commissioned from 1980 to 1985.

The *Hermes* and *Invincible* embarked on the long voyage to the Falklands from Portsmouth, England, on April 4, 1982, and the fighting escalated seriously the following month. The Falklands were within range of Argentine land-based aircraft; for the British, the major concern was the number of aircraft the Royal Navy could deploy. The *Hermes* carried sixteen Vertical Short Takeoff and Landing (VSTOL) Sea Harrier

FRS.1 attack aircraft of the Fleet Air Arm and ten Harrier GR.3 ground-attack planes of the Royal Air Force, along with ten Sea King helicopters. The *Invincible* carried eight Sea Harriers and ten Sea Kings. To assist the VSTOL Harriers in takeoff, the *Invincible*-class carriers were constructed with upward-sloping flight decks nicknamed ski-jump ramps.

Argentine planes actually sank two British destroyers and two frigates, and the loss of either carrier would have seriously endangered the entire British operation. Ten Sea Harriers were destroyed before the war ended with a British victory on June 14, 1982. Without the ability of the Royal Navy to supply carrier air power, there would have been little the British government could do to reclaim the Falklands.

While carriers were continually deployed around the world during the post-Vietnam era and into the 1980s, modernization efforts in both the carriers themselves and the aircraft that operated from their decks were ongoing despite periodic defense budget austerity and opposition. The aircraft carrier had validated its existence and in the process retained its preeminence on the high seas.

Returning to its homeport of Portsmouth following the British victory in the Falklands War of 1982, the Royal Navy aircraft carrier HMS *Invincible* is greeted by fireboats, tugs, and pleasure craft. The lead ship of a class of twenty-two-thousand-ton light aircraft carriers, the *Invincible* was decommissioned in 2005.

Defence Imagery photo

A British Aerospace Sea Harrier multi-role attack aircraft launches from the ski-jump ramp on the flight deck of the HMS *Hermes* during the Falklands War of 1982. The last of the British Royal Navy's *Centaur*-class aircraft carriers, the *Hermes* was commissioned in November 1959 and sold to the Indian navy in 1986. *IWM/Getty Images*

IN RETRIBUTION AND RELIEF

On August 2, 1990, the same day that Iraqi dictator Saddam Hussein sent his army to invade neighboring Kuwait, the USS *Independence* carrier strike group was ordered into the Arabian Sea to bolster the US presence in the troubled Middle East.

The initial American response to the Iraqi aggression was standard procedure. It was naval. A week after the orders were transmitted to the *Independence* group, the Egyptian government granted permission for the carrier *Dwight D. Eisenhower* to transit the Suez Canal into the Red Sea. Simultaneously, the *Saratoga* strike group, the battleship *Wisconsin*, and the helicopter assault carrier USS *Inchon*, with a battalion of combat-ready US Marines, headed for the region.

Aircraft fly over *Nimitz*-class carrier USS *Dwight D. Eisenhower* on July 10, 2012. *Dwight D. Eisenhower* was among the first US warships to enter the Red Sea upon the Iraqi invasion of Kuwait in August 1990. *US Navy photo/Mass Communication Specialist 2nd Class Julia A. Casper*

The *Nimitz*-class aircraft carrier USS *George H. W. Bush* lies under construction in Northrop Grumman Dry Dock 12 in Newport News, Virginia. Construction began on the *George H. W. Bush*, the last of the ten *Nimitz*-class carriers, in 2003, and the warship was commissioned in January 2009. Note the scrawled initials and messages left by workers on the section of the bulbous bow in the foreground. *US Navy photo*

Rapidly and characteristically, the US Navy, its supercarriers at the tip of the spear, drew a cordon of air and surface assets around Iraq and its ill-gotten gain. In time, the greatest sealift since the Vietnam War and the collective outrage of the world assembled a concentration of military force the likes of which had never been seen on Earth. Again proving themselves to be the most efficient means of transporting sustainable air assets to a potential combat zone, the aircraft carriers of the US Navy were destined to play a critical role in the buildup of coalition forces and the unleashing of offensive power that ejected Hussein's army from Kuwait.

When Operation Desert Storm, as it came to be known, commenced, six US carriers were on station in the Persian Gulf region, including the *Theodore Roosevelt*, *America*, *John F. Kennedy*, and *Saratoga* in the Red Sea, along with the *Ranger* and the thirty-six-year-old *Midway* in the Persian Gulf. Altogether, the carriers were capable of putting more than three hundred planes and myriad ordnance, conventional bombs, missiles, and high-tech "smart" weapons of the day into the air.

Naval air power contributed to the round-the-clock bombardment of Iraqi forces in a thirty-nine-day air campaign that heavily degraded the enemy prior to the opening of

the ground phase of Desert Storm on February 24, 1991. After the one-hundred-hour ground campaign ended with a decisive victory, naval aircraft were estimated to have flown approximately 40 percent of the combat sorties during the massive military undertaking. Eighteen nations contributed to the overwhelming naval power of the Desert Storm coalition, eradicating the Iraqi navy in surface and air action.

Despite the thorough nature of the victory and the role of the aircraft carriers in it, navy pilots paid a price. Lieutenant Scott Speicher became the first American casualty of the Gulf War when his F/A-18 Hornet was shot down by an Iraqi surface-to-air missile on the first night of Desert Storm. Lieutenant Jeffrey Zaun, piloting an A-6 Intruder, was shot down, paraded in front of Iraqi television cameras, and held captive for forty-seven days before his release. Both pilots flew from the carrier *Saratoga*.

While conventionally powered carriers provided most of the muscle for Desert Shield and Desert Storm, construction of the *Nimitz*-class nuclear carriers spanned five decades from the design of the lead ship to the commissioning of the *George H. W. Bush*, the last of ten in the class, in 2009. Meanwhile, the last of the US Navy's conventionally powered carriers, the

continued on page 202

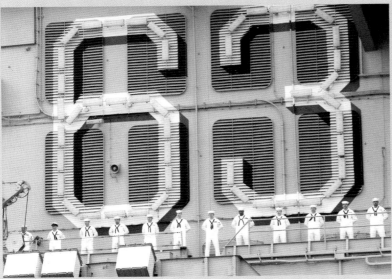

Above: During Operation Desert Shield, the buildup of overwhelming coalition forces on land, sea, and air that were unleashed in the subsequent Operation Desert Storm, a pair of McDonnell Douglas F/A-18 Hornet multi-role combat aircraft streak high above a US Navy aircraft carrier. More F/A-18s and several Grumman F-14 Tomcat air superiority fighters are visible on the carrier's deck. *Department of Defense photo*

Left: US Navy sailors stand at parade rest beneath the large recognition numbers emblazoned on the island of the USS *Kitty Hawk*, the last of the navy's conventionally powered carriers. Thirteen of its forty-eight years of service were spent with the navy's only forward-deployed carrier strike group based at Yokosuka, Japan. During its career, the *Kitty Hawk* deployed for combat operations in the Vietnam War in the 1960s and in Operation Enduring Freedom in 2001. *US Navy photo*

Right: The aircraft carrier USS *Kitty Hawk* is shown during operations at sea in company with other US Navy warships. The *Kitty Hawk* was decommissioned in 2009 after nearly a half-century of service. McDonnell Douglas F/A-18 Hornet strike aircraft are among the planes on the flight deck, while flight crewmen in their distinctive colored jerseys gather at the deck's forward edge. *US Navy photo*

Above: A variety of US Navy fixed-wing aircraft and helicopters sit on the flight deck of the *Nimitz*-class aircraft carrier USS *George Washington* in the harbor at Yokosuka, Japan. Commissioned on Independence Day, July 4, 1992, the *George Washington* relieved USS *Kitty Hawk* as the principal warship of the navy's only forward-deployed carrier strike group at Yokosuka in 2008. *US Navy photo*

Right: The immense size of a *Nimitz*-class aircraft carrier and its labyrinth of passages and spaces are readily apparent in this nocturnal image of the last of the class, the USS *George H. W. Bush*, under construction in Dry Dock 12 at the Northrop Grumman yards in Newport News, Virginia. Dry Dock 12 is the largest facility of its kind in the Western Hemisphere. The *George H. W. Bush* was assembled in sections during a six-year construction period and was completed at a cost of $6.2 billion. *US Navy photo*

Opposite left: A surgeon and technician perform an operation in the shipboard hospital of a US Navy aircraft carrier. The hospital aboard a *Nimitz*-class aircraft carrier includes fifty-three beds along with surgical suites. Six doctors, five dentists, and numerous nurses and technicians comprise the carrier's medical staff. *US Navy photo*

Opposite right: A cook aboard the *Nimitz*-class aircraft carrier USS *John C. Stennis* slices turkey for a Thanksgiving dinner for the ship's crew. During deployments, the *Nimitz*-class carriers transport enough refrigerated and dried provisions to feed six thousand people for seventy days without replenishment. *US Navy photo*

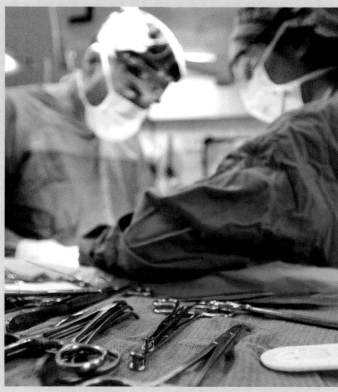

IN RETRIBUTION AND RELIEF

Above: Responding to signals from a flight deck crewman aboard the *Nimitz*-class aircraft carrier USS *George H. W. Bush*, a pilot of Strike Fighter Squadron VFA-15 based at Naval Air Station Oceana in Virginia Beach, Virginia, prepares to take off in his McDonnell Douglas F/A-18 Hornet multi-role fighter and combat aircraft. *US Navy photo*

Opposite: Flight deck crewmen guide a McDonnell Douglas F/A-18 Hornet into position for a catapult launch aboard the *Nimitz*-class aircraft carrier USS *Theodore Roosevelt*. The yellow jersey designates this crewman's responsibility as an aircraft handling officer. *Department of Defense photo*

continued from page 196

USS *Kitty Hawk*, was decommissioned in the same year. After serving thirteen years with the navy's only forward-deployed carrier strike group based at Yokosuka, Japan, *Kitty Hawk* was replaced by USS *George Washington* in 2008, and in turn the USS *Ronald Reagan* was slated to relieve the *George Washington* at Yokosuka in 2014.

The *Nimitz*-class carriers are engineering marvels. Designed for estimated service lives of fifty years, their two nuclear reactors are expected to require only one refueling—during the respective carriers' midlife complex overhauls at Newport News. The height of a *Nimitz* carrier is 244 feet from keel to mast, the equivalent of a twenty-four-story building. Each carrier has more than three thousand televisions and 2,500 telephones on board and an air-conditioning capacity of 2,250 tons—enough to cool more than five hundred homes. The shipboard hospital is equipped with state-of-the-art medical equipment and fifty-three beds with six medical doctors, a host of nursing personnel, and five dentists. When deployed, the carriers transport enough dried and refrigerated food to feed six thousand people for seventy days. Each year

Left: Crewmen wearing their color-coded jerseys swab the flight deck of the *Nimitz*-class aircraft carrier USS *Ronald Reagan*. Constructed by Northrop Grumman at Newport News, Virginia, the *Ronald Reagan* was launched in March 2001 and commissioned in July 2003. In 2014, the carrier was slated to relieve the USS *George Washington* in forward deployment with the Seventh Fleet carrier strike group based at Yokosuka, Japan. The *Ronald Reagan* previously deployed during Operation Iraqi Freedom and Operation Enduring Freedom. *US Navy photo*

Opposite: A Sikorsky SH-60 Seahawk helicopter hovers above the flight deck of the *Nimitz*-class aircraft carrier USS *Theodore Roosevelt*, the first carrier constructed by the welding of modular sections, leading a sub-class with minor structural alterations and better protection for ordnance storage areas. Commissioned on October 25, 1986, the *Theodore Roosevelt* deployed during the Gulf War and Operation Enduring Freedom. *Department of Defense photo*

Below: Sailors dressed in winter clothing clear snow from the flight deck of the USS *Nimitz*, the lead ship of ten nuclear-powered US Navy carriers that were constructed with an expected service life of fifty years or more. The *Nimitz* was launched in May 1972 and commissioned in 1975. The *Nimitz*-class carriers are required to refuel only once, during complex overhauls approximately twenty-five years after entering service. *US Navy photo*

more than one million pounds of mail are processed through a *Nimitz*-class carrier's post office.

The three Nimitz carrier sub-classes are distinguishable by outwardly subtle design and equipment changes. Commissioned in 1986, the *Theodore Roosevelt* was the first carrier constructed by the welding of modular sections, leading a sub-class with minor structural alterations and better protection for ordnance storage areas. With the *Ronald Reagan* and *George H. W. Bush*, the two carriers of the *Ronald Reagan*

subclass, certain cost-saving and innovative design elements are common, including a reconfigured island. The *George H. W. Bush* was completed with some features of the coming *Gerald R. Ford* class, including upgrades to radar and other electronic and environmental equipment, a bulbous bow design, and improved propellers. While the majority of the *Nimitz*-class carriers have been completed for an approximate cost of $4.5 billion, the final price tag for the *George H. W. Bush* was roughly $6.2 billion.

Festooned with bunting, the island of the nuclear-powered aircraft carrier USS *Gerald R. Ford* is suspended above the flight deck prior to ceremonies in 2012 to mark its installation at the Huntington Ingalls yards in Norfolk, Virginia. The *Gerald R. Ford* is the first of a class of ten nuclear-powered carriers that are expected to replace the retiring warships of the *Nimitz* class. Two other proposed carriers of the *Gerald R. Ford* class, USS *John F. Kennedy* and USS *Enterprise*, have been named. *US Navy photo*

As the last carriers of the *Nimitz* class were being completed at Newport News, plans moved forward for the construction of the next generation of aircraft carrier: a platform that would extend the role of the US Navy's capital ship well beyond the mid-twenty-first century. With an estimated construction cost of $12.8 billion, the *Gerald R. Ford*–class aircraft carriers represent the first wholly redesigned warships of their kind since the *Nimitz* carriers were conceived in the mid-1960s.

Although their high cost has given members of Congress, and indeed the American public, reason to pause, the *Ford*-class carriers are expected to provide long-term savings in future defense budgets. During their estimated fifty-year service lives, each of the three planned carriers is expected to save $4 billion in maintenance, upkeep, and operational costs derived from a reduction of seven hundred crewmembers from the *Nimitz*-class ships, a four hundred-man reduction in necessary air wing personnel, and the introduction of electric utilities that

eliminate the need for steam generation and piping and reduce maintenance requirements and surface corrosion.

Further, the latest technology is being employed throughout, including the new A1B nuclear reactor, a smaller and more efficient design that supplies more than three times the electrical power of the A4W reactors in the *Nimitz*-class carriers. The Electromagnetic Aircraft Launch System (EMALS) utilizes a linear motor drive rather than a steam-piston system to launch aircraft, while the Advanced Arresting Gear (AAG) system is a modular integration of energy absorbers and power conditioning equipment that replaces the existing Mark 7 arrester gear on the *Nimitz* carriers.

Perhaps the most impressive feature of the *Ford*-class carriers is their anticipated ability to maximize the capabilities of their carrier air wings—the raison d'être for the aircraft carrier. The new carriers' systems are designed to optimize the sortie generation rate (SGR), putting planes in the air at a 33 percent higher efficiency than their *Nimitz*-class predecessors.

The nuclear-powered aircraft carrier USS *Gerald R. Ford* lies in dry dock at the Huntington Ingalls (formerly Northrop Grumman) yards in Newport News, Virginia. The *Gerald R. Ford* was launched in November 2013 and slated for commissioning in 2016. Displacing 110,000 tons, the *Gerald R. Ford*-class carriers are the largest warships of their kind ever built. *US Navy photo*

The US Navy ordered the lead ship of the *Gerald R. Ford* class from Newport News Shipbuilding on September 10, 2008. She was laid down on November 13, 2009, and launched on November 9, 2013; delivery is expected in the spring of 2016. Two additional carriers, the *John F. Kennedy* and the *Enterprise*, are planned. The new carriers will be 1,092 feet long with a beam of 256 feet at the flight deck, and a height from waterline to mast of nearly 250 feet. They will displace more than 110,000 tons fully loaded, and their nuclear powerplants will generate a top speed of more than thirty knots. Each ship's complement and air wing is expected to total more than 4,500 personnel and at least seventy-five aircraft.

Much of the new equipment and the systems aboard the *Ford*-class carriers owe their evolution to testing that took place aboard the decommissioned USS *America* during the spring of 1995. Amid protests from groups wanting to preserve the carrier as a museum, the USS *America* was used in live-fire testing to aid in the design of future aircraft carriers. Subjected

to underwater explosions and other stresses, the *America* was sunk after the evaluation was complete.

During the naming ceremony for the USS *Gerald R. Ford* on January 16, 2007, the late president's daughter, Susan Ford Bales, linked the carriers and their crews. "The USS *Gerald R. Ford* also shares a unique bond with another ship and her crew," she remarked. "As many of you know, several years ago the USS *America* was towed into the Atlantic Ocean and then sunk in a series of tests to verify critical components of the CVN-78 carrier program. Those tests were essential to maximizing the survivability of the future carrier fleet, including CVN-78. The USS *America* and her proud crew set a magnificent example of patriotism and unwavering service to the US Navy. And now their valor lives on within the spirit of the USS *Gerald R. Ford*. For that gift and for their service, we are deeply grateful to the *America* and her crew."

When President Bill Clinton stepped to the microphone aboard the USS *Theodore Roosevelt* in 1993, he described the

Above: A trio of flight deck crewmen relaxes in conversation aboard the *Nimitz*-class aircraft carrier USS *Theodore Roosevelt* in this photo taken at twilight during a deployment. The aircraft parked on the flight deck are Grumman F-14 Tomcat fighters. *US Navy photo*

Right: Flight deck crewmen aboard the *Nimitz*-class aircraft carrier USS *Theodore Roosevelt* direct a Grumman F-14 Tomcat air superiority fighter to a catapult position during flight operations at sea. The F-14 served as the US Navy's frontline carrier-based fighter from 1974 through 2006. *US Navy photo*

Above left: The air boss controls flight operations on both the flight and hangar decks of a US Navy aircraft carrier. Air bosses usually wear the yellow jersey of aircraft handling officers but may choose another color depending on the operational context. *US Navy photo*

Above right: Captain Kevin O'Flaherty, the executive officer of the nuclear-powered *Nimitz*-class aircraft carrier USS *Abraham Lincoln*, communicates with other personnel and reviews reports on the ship's bridge. The executive officer generally fulfills the role of the carrier's second in command. *US Navy photo*

role of the carrier and the navy as an instrument of US foreign policy. "When word of crisis breaks out in Washington," said the president, "it's no accident that the first question that comes to everyone's lips is, 'Where is the nearest carrier?'"

In war and peace, the US Navy is a first responder, and the heart of its response is the carrier strike group. The US Navy fleet response plan specifies that six carrier strike groups remain either deployed or prepared to deploy within thirty days at all times while two additional groups must be deployable within ninety days. Capable of delivering military might or rendering humanitarian aid when either is necessary, the carrier strike group is composed of a carrier and its accompanying air wing, one or more *Ticonderoga*-class guided-missile cruisers, a squadron of two or three *Arleigh Burke*–class guided-missile destroyers, a pair of *Los Angeles*–class attack submarines, and a logistical support ship. The escorting warships and submarines are multi-mission capable, armed with air and antisubmarine defense systems and the strike capability of Tomahawk cruise missiles.

Previously known as carrier battle groups, these task forces were officially renamed carrier strike groups in the autumn of 2004. At any given time the US Navy operates up to eleven carrier strike groups, including the single forward-based strike group at Yokosuka, Japan. The broadly defined mission of the carrier strike group is to conduct centralized planning, integration, coordination, and control of its offensive and defensive assets in support of a variety of activities in the air and on land and sea. These include direct-strike missions and electronic, antisubmarine, antimine, and amphibious operations.

Modern aircraft carriers have often been generically referred to as "floating cities." Indeed, much like a city, a carrier is self-sustainable for an extended period of time. The commanding officer, usually holding the rank of captain and qualified as a naval aviator, directs operations through more than a dozen areas of responsibility, or departments. These include administration, air, aircraft intermediate maintenance, medical, navigation, operations, engineering, communications, weapons, supply, engineering, training, and others. Deployed carrier air wings operate in a functionally similar manner to the carrier's organization. The carrier air wing commander is responsible for all aspects of air wing operations and works in tandem with the carrier commander. Among the commander's areas of responsibility are operations, undersea warfare, air intelligence, weapons, and maintenance.

During normal operations, several key individuals are on the bridge, the primary area of control for all functions at sea, at all times. The officer of the deck is responsible for navigation, communications, and executing specific plans for the day, while the quartermaster of the watch assists with navigation and maintains the ship's log. The boatswain's mate of the watch supervises a group of sailors including the helmsman, who steers the ship; the lee helmsman, who relays speed and engine control information; and the lookouts.

Primary Flight Control, commonly known as "Pri-Fly," is the nerve center of flight operations aboard the carrier and equivalent to the control tower of a standard airport. The air officer, routinely known as the "air boss," and his assistant, the "mini boss," control aircraft operations throughout the carrier flight deck and hangar deck and monitor aircraft in flight up to a distance of five nautical miles. Others with specific roles include the catapult officer, aircraft handling officer, landing signal officer, arresting gear officer, and aircraft directors, among others. In the highly choreographed flight operations, each responsible group wears a colored jersey that readily identifies its members' role in takeoff, recovery, movement, ordnance, and other critical areas.

While the US Navy is by far the leading naval force in the world in terms of aircraft carrier development and deployment, numerous navies around the globe have commissioned aircraft carriers in service while others are evaluating their own investment in the warships. Currently, the United States, Great Britain, France, Australia, China, Russia, Thailand, Brazil, Japan, South Korea, Spain, Turkey, Italy, and India operate true aircraft carriers capable of launching and recovering some type of aircraft.

The British Royal Navy has long been an innovator in terms of design and construction. Angled flight decks, steam catapults, mirrored landing sites, ski-jump ramps, and other innovations originated with British carriers. The last of the Royal Navy's twenty-two-thousand-ton *Invincible*-class carriers, HMS *Illustrious*, was withdrawn from service in 2014, and temporarily the British are without a fully operational fleet aircraft carrier. Plans to build a class of large carriers for the Royal Navy were canceled in the mid-1960s. However, three decades later, it became apparent that a new generation of aircraft carrier was necessary. In the spring of 1998, a government-sponsored Strategic Defence Review noted that carriers provide the "capability to operate offensive aircraft when foreign basing may be denied; all required space and infrastructure—where foreign bases are available they are not always available early in

a conflict and infrastructure is often lacking; and a coercive and deterrent effect when deployed to a trouble spot."

The report concluded with a resounding endorsement for carrier construction, stating, "The emphasis is now on increased offensive air power and the ability to operate the largest possible range of aircraft in the widest possible range of roles. When the current carrier force reaches the end of its planned life, we plan to replace it with two larger vessels. Work will now begin to refine our requirements, but present thinking suggests that they might be of the order of 30,000–40,000 tonnes [33,600–44,800 tons] and capable of deploying up to fifty aircraft, including helicopters."

The two planned aircraft carriers began to take conceptual shape, with the resulting 65,000-ton *Queen Elizabeth* class now under construction. When completed, the two carriers of the class will be the largest warships ever built in the United Kingdom. The lead ship was ordered on May 20, 2008, laid down on July 7, 2009, and launched on July 17, 2014. Completion is expected sometime in 2017. The *Queen Elizabeth* was assembled at Rosyth Dockyard in the Firth of Forth from nine modules constructed at six different shipyards. The second carrier, HMS *Prince of Wales*, was laid down on May 26, 2011, with launching planned for 2017 and commissioning for 2020. At the end of 2014, construction on the *Prince of Wales* was about 40 percent complete.

Both carriers are powered by a pair of massive Rolls-Royce MT30 gas turbines along with four Wärtsilä diesel generator sets that allow a top speed of more than twenty-five knots. Nuclear power was considered but discounted due to its high cost. Each carrier's superstructure is divided into two structures, a forward island for navigation and an aft island that contains the flying control center, or "flyco."

The *Queen Elizabeth*–class carriers are designed for standard catapult and arrestor gear flight operations; however, the carriers are not equipped with them at this time. Therefore, the standard air complement will include forty aircraft: Lockheed Martin F-35B Lightning II STOVL (short takeoff, vertical landing) multi-role fighters and a combination of rotary aircraft such as the AgustaWestland AW101 Merlin medium lift, AW159 battlefield utility, Boeing Chinook tandem rotor, and AW Apache (license-built versions of the Boeing AH-64 Apache Longbow) attack helicopters.

Outside the US Navy, the only operational nuclear-powered aircraft carrier in the world is the French *Charles de Gaulle*, displacing thirty-eight thousand tons. Ordered in 1986, the *Charles de Gaulle* was laid down in April 1989, launched in May

continued on page 216

Opposite: The aft island of the HMS *Queen Elizabeth* sits ready for installation at Rosyth Dock in the Firth of Forth. The sixty-five-thousand-ton carrier is the first of its class, and completion is expected sometime in 2017. The conventionally powered *Queen Elizabeth* and the second carrier of the class, HMS *Prince of Wales*, are the first new aircraft carriers of the British Royal Navy in decades. © Kenny Williamson/Alamy Live News

Streaming patriotic contrails, aircraft of the British Royal Air Force Red Arrow flight demonstration team streak past the HMS *Queen Elizabeth* during ceremonies marking a milestone in the carrier's construction. The *Queen Elizabeth* was launched in July 2014 and slated for commissioning in early 2016. *© Department of Defense photo/Alamy*

continued from page 210

1994, and commissioned on May 18, 2001. Originally named *Richelieu*, the carrier was renamed for the foremost French president, general, and statesman of the twentieth century after a vigorous debate among lawmakers in Paris. The *Charles de Gaulle* underwent sea trials in 1999 and, as a result, the flight deck was slightly lengthened to allow the Northrop Grumman E-2C Hawkeye airborne early warning aircraft to operate efficiently. A broken propeller blade delayed formal commissioning for about five months. Work was halted four times during construction, and the eventual cost topped $3.5 billion. The carrier is powered by two PWR (pressurized water reactor) Type K15 nuclear reactors and Alstom 61MW turbines that generate a top speed of more than twenty-seven knots. It is capable of five years of continuous sailing time at twenty-five knots without refueling. Its flight deck is nearly 640 feet long, and its overall length is 858 feet with a beam of just over 211 feet.

The *Charles de Gaulle* carries up to forty aircraft, including the Dassault-Breguet Super Étendard attack plane, the Dassault Rafale multi-role fighter, the E-2C, and the Eurocopter AS565 Panther or NHIndustries NH90 medium transport helicopters. The carrier incorporates the SYTEX command and control system developed by the Thales Group, and air defenses include the SAAM (surface anti-air missile system) from Eurosam, which is effective against aircraft and anti-ship missiles, and eight Nexter 20F2 twenty-millimeter guns. Plans for a second French aircraft carrier have been shelved. If revived, the project would constitute a new class of warship.

After World War II, the French navy reemerged on the world stage with the *Arromanches*, a carrier that began its career as the HMS *Colossus*. After serving with the Royal Navy in the Pacific, the carrier was loaned to the French navy in 1946 and then purchased in 1951. The *Arromanches* participated in the First Indochina War and the Suez Crisis, was later converted to an antisubmarine warfare carrier, and was then sold for scrap in 1978.

During the 1950s, the US *Independence*-class light carriers *Belleau Wood* and *Langley* were transferred to the French navy under the Mutual Defense Assistance Act. There, they were renamed the *Bois Belleau* and *La Fayette*, respectively, and served for several years before they were returned to the US Navy and sold for scrap.

The first post–World War II aircraft carriers of the French navy were the *Clemenceau* and *Foch*, each displacing more than

Above: Formerly in service with the British Royal Navy as HMS *Colossus*, the renamed *Arromanches* became France's first post–World War II aircraft carrier. The *Arromanches* participated in the First Indochina War and the Suez Crisis of 1956. Later converted to an antisubmarine warfare vessel, the carrier was scrapped in 1978. *National Naval Aviation Museum/Robert L. Lawson Photograph Collection/1996.488.037.056*

Previous pages: The world's only operational nuclear-powered aircraft carrier outside the US Navy, the French carrier *Charles de Gaulle* lies at anchor in the Mediterranean port of Toulon. The thirty-eight-thousand-ton *Charles de Gaulle* was launched in 1994 and commissioned in 2001 after a broken propeller delayed the ceremony for five months. *© Brian Jannsen/Alamy*

The daily routine of life aboard an aircraft carrier is highly regimented for the more than five thousand sailors and airmen who call the ship home for extended periods of time. Assigned to specific roles aboard the ship, from cooking and serving meals to navigating the waters of the globe and writing news releases for the media, some percentage of a carrier's personnel are active all day, every day.

Those who are assigned to certain internal areas, such as the mechanical rooms and even the hangar deck, may go days without heading topside and seeing daylight. Space is at a premium, and stairs that connect one deck to another are nearly vertical, requiring some amount of practice to climb with ease. While officers are usually provided with their own cabins, enlisted sailors share berthing compartments with up to sixty others and sleep in racks stacked three high.

Individuals stow their personal belongings in small bins and lockers. The sailors in each compartment share bathroom facilities and a common area outfitted with a television that receives a satellite signal. Sailors are provided with some diversions, such as satellite telephones to keep in touch with family and friends while on a prolonged deployment.

The extensive laundry on the latest *Nimitz*–class carriers includes nine heavy-duty washers, two small washers for special items, eleven dryers, and twelve steam presses. Several galleys operate daily, providing meals for the ship's complement of more than 3,000 sailors and the 2,500 personnel of the assigned carrier air wing.

Working flight deck control aboard the *Nimitz*-class aircraft carrier USS *Harry S. Truman*, a sailor positions aircraft in preparation for upcoming operations. The locations of aircraft and vehicles are critical to the efficiency of flight operations and the safety of the personnel involved. *US Navy photo*

Above: Six Dassault Super Étendard carrier-borne strike fighters sit on the flight deck of the French aircraft carrier *Foch*. Launched in July 1960, the *Foch* displaced twenty-two thousands tons and deployed during the Lebanese Civil War, Libyan provocations in the Gulf of Sidra, and the Balkan wars of the 1990s before being sold to the Brazilian navy in 2000 and renamed the *São Paulo*. © *NU Collection/Alamy*

Opposite above: The twenty-seven-thousand-ton Italian aircraft carrier *Conte di Cavour* lies moored in harbor while visitors come aboard. The carrier was commissioned in 2008 with a complement of up to thirty aircraft. In 2010, the *Conte di Cavour* was deployed to Haiti to participate in earthquake relief efforts in that stricken island nation. © *Gaetano56/Creative Commons/CC BY-SA 3.0*

Opposite below: The Italian aircraft carrier *Giuseppe Garibaldi* and the Turkish frigate *Gediz* steam through Atlantic waters during Operation Majestic Eagle, a multinational NATO exercise conducted off the coast of Morocco in 2004. The *Giuseppe Garibaldi* was commissioned in 1985 and later converted to an antisubmarine warfare carrier. *US Navy photo*

twenty-two thousand standard tons. The *Clemenceau* was laid down at the Brest shipyard in November 1955, launched two years later, and commissioned on November 22, 1961, as the lead ship of its class. Through the years, its air complement included up to forty aircraft, among them the French Dassault Étendard IV fighter and Dassault-Breguet Super Étendard attack aircraft, along with the American-built Vought F-8 Crusader fighter.

The *Clemenceau* deployed during testing for French nuclear weapons in the 1960s, the Lebanese Civil War from 1982 to 1984, the Iran-Iraq War of the late 1980s, the unrest in the Balkans, and Operations Desert Shield and Desert Storm. After thirty-six years of service, she was decommissioned in 1997 and later scrapped.

The *Foch* was launched in July 1960, commissioned three years later, and deployed to the Mediterranean during the Lebanese Civil War, the tensions with Libya related to free passage in the Gulf of Sidra, and the unrest in the Balkans. When the US Navy declined to cooperate with the makers of the feature film *Crimson Tide*, scenes were shot aboard the *Foch*. The carrier was sold to the Brazilian navy in 2000, was renamed the *São Paulo*, and remains in service.

In 2008, the Italian navy commissioned the twenty-seven-thousand-ton aircraft carrier *Conti di Cavour*, powered by six diesel engines with four General Electric gas turbines that produce eighty-eight thousand shaft horsepower and a top speed of twenty-eight knots. The *Cavour* carries up to thirty aircraft but typically has fewer aboard. These include eight AV8B Harrier VSTOL jump jets and a dozen AgustaWestland EH101 Merlin helicopters used for airborne early warning. The Italians also operate the smaller 11,300-ton carrier *Giuseppe Garibaldi*, commissioned in 1985 and now designated an antisubmarine warfare carrier with eighteen aircraft, Harrier attack planes, and Agusta SH-3D antisubmarine helicopters that are license-built versions of the Sikorsky Sea King.

The Soviet (and later the Russian) concept of the aircraft carrier is somewhat different than that of Western nations. The Soviets built two *Moskva*-class helicopter carriers in the 1960s and then designed aircraft-carrying missile cruisers commissioned from 1975 to 1990. Although they have been capable of carrying a robust number of rotary and fixed-wing aircraft and are generally classified as aircraft carriers in the West, the Russians have considered these warships as aircraft-carrying cruisers due to their primary roles of support for ballistic missile submarines, surface ships, and aircraft equipped with anti-ship missiles rather than as global projectors of air power.

Above: Launched in 1972 and commissioned three years later, the Soviet navy's *Kiev* was classified by most Western analysts as an aircraft carrier. However, the Soviets more aptly described the 30,520-ton warship as an aircraft-carrying missile cruiser. Following the fall of the Soviet Union, the Russian government decommissioned the *Kiev* in 1993 and eventually sold the vessel to China. This aerial view was taken from the ship's port quarter. *Department of Defense photo*

Opposite: Yakovlev Yak-38 "Forger" strike fighters, the only vertical takeoff and landing (VTOL) aircraft of the Soviet navy, sit on the flight deck of the aircraft-carrying missile cruiser *Minsk*. The *Kiev*-class *Minsk* was commissioned into the Soviet navy in 1978, decommissioned in 1993, and later sold to China. *Department of Defense photo*

The lead ship of the *Kiev*-class aircraft-carrying missile cruisers was laid down at the Chernomorskiy shipyard in southern Ukraine in 1970, launched in 1972, and commissioned in December 1975. The *Kiev* displaced 30,530 tons and was powered by four steam turbines that generated 140,000 shaft horsepower and a top speed of thirty-two knots. Its aircraft complement totaled up to thirty-two planes and helicopters, including the Yakovlev Yak-38 vertical takeoff and landing (VTOL) strike fighter and the Kamov Ka-25 or Ka-27 antisubmarine helicopters.

The *Kiev* served as a flagship of the Soviet fleet and participated in numerous exercises; however, with the decline and fall of the Soviet Union the ship fell into disrepair and was decommissioned in 1993. It was eventually sold to Binhai Aircraft Park in Tianjin, China, and redeveloped as a tourist attraction and luxury hotel. Three other *Kiev*-class ships—the *Minsk*, *Admiral Gorshkov*, and *Novorossiysk*—were completed.

Minsk and *Novorossiysk* were decommissioned in 1993, and *Admiral Gorshkov* was sold to India and renamed *Vikramaditya*.

One of two intended aircraft-carrying missile cruisers of its class, the *Admiral Kuznetsov* is the only operational ship of its kind in the Russian navy today. She was ordered in the spring of 1991, laid down at the Black Sea shipyard in Mykolaiv, Ukraine, in April 1982, and commissioned in December 1990. Displacing forty-three thousand tons with an overall length of 1,001 feet and a beam of 236 feet, the carrier is powered by eight turbo-pressurized boilers and steam turbines that produce two hundred thousand shaft horsepower and a top speed of twenty-nine knots.

The *Admiral Kuznetsov* carries up to fifty-two aircraft, including the Sukhoi Su-33 air-superiority fighter, the Mikoyan MiG-29 multipurpose fighter, the Sukhoi Su-25 close air-support plane, and the Kamov Ka-27 helicopter equipped for multiple roles. Fixed-wing aircraft are launched

Above: A Sukhoi Su-27 "Flanker" naval strike fighter is serviced on the flight deck of the Russian aircraft-carrying missile cruiser *Admiral Kuznetsov*. The *Admiral Kuznetsov* was commissioned in December 1990 and is the only active warship of its kind in the Russian navy today. She carries up to fifty-two aircraft of various types. © *ITAR-TASS Photo Agency/Alamy*

Opposite: *Daring*-class air defense destroyer HMS *Dragon* of the British Royal Navy (foreground) shadows Russian aircraft-carrying missile cruiser *Admiral Kuznetsov* in the spring of 2014. This photograph was taken as the *Admiral Kuznetsov* led a task group into the English Channel off the coast of the French port city of Brest. *Royal Navy photo*

with the assistance of a ski-jump ramp. Although costs have limited operations, the *Admiral Kuznetsov* has participated in numerous exercises in waters near the Arctic Circle and in the Mediterranean. After a quarter century of service, she is due for an extensive refit. With the anticipated overhaul, the ship is expected to serve until 2030.

A second carrier of the *Admiral Kuznetsov* class, the *Varyag* was under construction during the collapse of the Soviet Union, and the Ukrainian government sold the hull to China, which in turn completed it and commissioned the carrier *Liaoning*. A third ship, *Ulyanovsk*, was scrapped shortly after its keel was laid.

For several years, Western observers have noted a growing Soviet interest in the development of a supercarrier, but

economic and political uncertainty have terminated such projects. In the mid-1980s, the Soviets ordered the supercarrier *Ulyanovsk*, intended to be the first of its class. Its keel was laid in November 1988, but three years later the hull was scrapped at just 20 percent complete and a second carrier was canceled. With a standard displacement of nearly seventy thousand tons, overall length of 1,030 feet, and beam of just over 275 feet, the *Ulyanov* would have been larger than the US Navy's *Forrestal*-class carriers but still smaller than those of the *Nimitz* class. It was projected to carry up to sixty-eight aircraft, including forty-four Su-33 and MiG-29 fighters, six Yakovlev Yak-44 early-warning aircraft, and eighteen Kamov Ka-27 helicopters.

There are indications that Russian interest in a supercarrier may have been revived recently, and speculation centers

Flight deck crewmen aboard the *Nimitz*-class aircraft carrier USS *Abraham Lincoln* assemble amid a broad spectrum of colored jerseys that designate their responsibilities during flight operations. Commissioned in November 1989, the *Abraham Lincoln* played an integral role in relief efforts following an earthquake that ravaged large areas of Indonesia in 2004. The carrier also deployed during Operation Iraqi Freedom and Operation Enduring Freedom. *US Navy photo*

THE COLORS OF FLIGHT OPERATIONS

Flight operations aboard a modern aircraft carrier require the seamless, perfectly choreographed efforts of a number of highly trained teams. At least eight teams are responsible for the preparation and execution of launches and recoveries aboard the carrier's deck, and each team member wears a distinctive colored jersey that denotes their specific function.

The air boss usually wears a yellow jersey but may choose to wear another color. Yellow designates the aircraft handling officers, plane directors who move aircraft on the flight and hangar decks, and catapult and arresting gear officers. Catapult and arresting gear crewmen, personnel involved in air wing maintenance and quality control, cargo handling, hook runners, photographer's mates, ground support equipment troubleshooters, and helicopter landing signal enlisted personnel wear green jerseys.

White jerseys indicate personnel responsible for quality assurance, safety observers, liquid oxygen crews, air transfer officers, landing signal officers, and squadron plane inspectors, while medical personnel wear white with a red cross emblazoned prominently. Ordnance personnel handling bombs, missiles, and ammunition as well as firefighters, explosive ordnance disposal personnel, and crash and salvage crews wear red. Plane handler trainees and inexperienced flight deck workers subordinate to those in yellow jerseys are recognized in blue along with messengers and phone communicators, tractor drivers, and aircraft elevator operators.

Aviation fuel handlers wear purple jerseys, while air wing plane captains, squadron personnel who prepare planes for flight, and air wing line-leading petty officers wear brown. The final checker, or inspector, wears either a black or a white jersey.

To a lesser degree, the pants worn during flight operations are also indicative of an individual's role. Khaki indicates an officer or chief petty officer, while petty officers and enlisted sailors wear navy blue pants.

around a warship that is actually larger than the *Nimitz*-class carriers, with an air wing of more than a hundred planes and helicopters. Russian media outlets have displayed a scale model of the proposed carrier, but it appears that the country's first attempt to construct a true aircraft carrier with force projection capabilities faces numerous challenges.

Currently, the Russian navy lists 270 active ships on its roster, but fewer than half of these are reported to be functional. Russian foreign policymakers have also lagged in the development of relationships with other countries that would provide port facilities. With the warming of relations between the United States and Cuba, the best opportunity to find a welcoming port in the Western Hemisphere might reside with Venezuela.

Above: The 67,500-ton *Liaoning*, the first operational aircraft carrier of the People's Republic of China's People's Liberation Army Navy Surface Force, lies moored at the Dalian shipyard in Liaoning Province, China. The *Liaoning* began its career as the *Admiral Kuznetsov*–class aircraft-carrying missile cruiser *Varyag* of the Soviet navy. However, with the collapse of the Soviet Union, the government of Ukraine sold the unfinished ship to China. © *epa European pressphoto agency b.v./Alamy*

Steam from the catapult launch of a jet aircraft shrouds flight operations crewmen on the deck of the *Nimitz*-class aircraft carrier USS *John C. Stennis*. Commissioned in December 1995, the *John C. Stennis* supported ground operations in Afghanistan in the spring of 2013 while leading a powerful US Navy carrier strike group. *US Navy photo*

One analyst recently wrote of Russia's carrier aspirations, "A supercarrier is not a means unto itself. It is a unit of investment. Building a supercarrier without a corresponding foreign policy and supportive foreign naval bases is like buying a multi-billion-dollar casino chip and not playing any of the games."

On the other hand, the People's Republic of China appears to be on a steady course to develop operational aircraft carriers, and some analysts speculate that the People's Liberation Army Navy (PLAN) plans as many as four carriers in the coming years. The *Liaoning*, the former Russian *Varyag*, is currently operating as a training carrier, according to Chinese sources, following an extensive refit that took an exhaustive fourteen years in the shipyards at Dalian.

The *Liaoning* completed sea trials in August 2012 and loaded Shenyang J-15 multi-role fighters to conduct flight trials that continued for two more years. The carrier's air complement is reported at thirty-two planes and helicopters, including the J-15, the Changhe Z-18 transport helicopter, the Kamov Ka-31 airborne early-warning helicopter, and the Harbin Z-9 utility helicopter.

Although the prospects for China to develop a real blue water naval aviation presence appear daunting, Deputy Navy Chief Adm. Song Xue said through the Chinese state-run news agency Xinhua, "We won't have just one [carrier]." The admiral also indicated that future carriers will transport a larger number of J-15 strike aircraft than the twenty-four aboard *Liaoning*. Still, the complexity of aircraft carrier construction and the necessary resources and training to develop multiple aircraft carriers would indicate that a substantial Chinese augmentation of carrier forces is years, if not decades, away. Nevertheless, continuous adversarial relations with the government of Taiwan, a simmering dispute with Japan over a group of islands in the East China Sea, and a desire to establish overseas bases in the Indian Ocean may have spurred the Chinese to see carrier air power as an instrument of foreign policy.

Truly, aircraft carriers remain a primary instrument in the protection of national interests for those nations who deploy them. In recent years, carriers have responded to global hotspots of civil war, genocide, terrorism, and interference with the maritime right of free passage for merchant shipping. As former Secretary of State William Cohen once said, "If you don't have that forward deployed presence, you have less of a voice, less of an influence."

When Al Qaeda terrorists struck the World Trade Center in New York City and the Pentagon in Washington, D.C., on September 11, 2001, the USS *Enterprise* was just completing a deployment in support of Operation Southern Watch, enforcing no-fly zones in Iraq. The carrier was heading south in the Indian Ocean, intending to return to its home port of Norfolk, Virginia. Without orders from a higher level, the *Enterprise* commander ordered a 180-degree turn and set a course for the Arabian Sea. For the next three weeks, the *Enterprise* conducted air operations in support of Operation Enduring Freedom, striking Taliban and Al Qaeda targets in Afghanistan with nearly seven hundred sorties.

The thirteen years of Operation Enduring Freedom, October 2001 through December 2014, tested the endurance of naval forces from numerous nations committed to victory in the war on terror. Strike aircraft flew thousand-mile round-trip missions from carrier decks in the Arabian Gulf to hit targets in Iraq and Afghanistan. During the first seventy-six days of Enduring Freedom, American aircraft flew more than 6,500 missions; 4,900 of these, roughly 75 percent, were flown by carrier-based naval pilots and air crewmen. By the first week of February 2002, US planes had flown more than twenty thousand sorties, half of them the work of naval aircraft.

When the *John C. Stennis* carrier strike group completed four months of air support for coalition ground troops in Afghanistan in March 2013, the pilots and crewmen of Carrier Air Wing 9 had completed 1,200 missions and 7,400 flight hours. "We have not missed a single mission and hit every target we aimed for on the first pass every time," declared Capt. Dell Bull, commander of the air wing. "It's the work of all of us, the air wing, the strike group, and the ship."

On December 1, 2001, a French naval task force including the *Charles de Gaulle*, the frigates *Jean Bart*, *Jean de Vienne*,

The *Nimitz*-class aircraft carrier USS *Harry S. Truman* and a support ship steam in open waters. Several McDonnell Douglas F/A-18 Hornet strike aircraft are parked forward on the flight deck, while Grumman F-14 Tomcat air superiority fighters are seen aft. The *Harry S. Truman* carrier strike group was among five deployed early in the 2003 Iraq War. *US Navy photo*

Following pages: A pair of McDonnell Douglas F/A-18 Hornet strike aircraft speed forward after launching from the deck of the nuclear-powered *Nimitz*-class aircraft carrier USS *John C. Stennis*. During Operation Enduring Freedom, the *John C. Stennis* carrier strike group provided air support for ground operations and participated in multinational fleet operations. *US Navy photo*

and *La Motte-Picquet*, the attack submarine *Rubis*, the tanker *Meuse*, and the aviso *Commandant Ducuing* sailed for the Arabian Sea. The Super Étendard strike aircraft, Rafale fighters, and surveillance aircraft aboard the *Charles de Gaulle* flew 140 missions, averaging twelve per day.

During the war in Kosovo in 1998 and 1999, a multinational naval force conducted air operations against

Above: Astronauts Gordon Cooper, Jr., (right) and Charles "Pete" Conrad, Jr., walk across the flight deck of the *Essex*-class aircraft carrier USS *Lake Champlain* after their recovery following an eight-day orbit of the Earth during the Gemini 5 space mission in August 1965. © *NG Images/Alamy*

Opposite: Vertical landing-capable British Aerospace Sea Harrier attack aircraft crowd the flight deck of the HMS *Invincible*. The versatile Harrier provided an edge for British forces during the Falklands War with Argentina in 1982. Prior to decommissioning in 2005, the *Invincible* served as the flagship of the Royal Navy and was deployed during unrest in the Balkans and the Iraq War of 2003. *Royal Navy photo*

Yugoslav forces. The British carrier HMS *Invincible*, the Italian *Giuseppe Garibaldi*, the US Navy's *Theodore Roosevelt* and amphibious assault ship *Kearsarge*, and the French carrier *Foch* were among those in service.

As US and coalition forces were marshaled to topple Iraqi dictator Saddam Hussein in the spring of 2003, the navy positioned five carrier strike groups in the region, led by the *Harry S. Truman* and *Theodore Roosevelt* in the eastern Mediterranean Sea and the *Kitty Hawk*, *Constellation*, and *Abraham Lincoln* in the Persian Gulf. Even prior to and after that conflict, the presence of an American aircraft carrier in the troubled region had been almost continuous.

Carrier-based aircraft completed a significant number of the air missions launched during Operation Iraqi Freedom. Before returning to its home port of San Diego, California, in the autumn of 2003, the carrier *Nimitz*, which had relieved the *Abraham Lincoln* on station in March, launched more than 6,500 sorties against the forces of Saddam Hussein

during its six-month deployment. Assigned to the *Nimitz* carrier strike group were the cruisers *Princeton* and *Chosin*, the ships of Destroyer Squadron 23, the frigate *Rodney M. Davis*, and the combat support ship USS *Bridge*. In a single month, US carriers launched more than seven thousand sorties, and in a single day the number of missions topped two hundred.

In spring 2011, the *Charles de Gaulle* launched air strikes against the army of Libyan dictator Muammar Qaddafi, enforcing a United Nations Security Council resolution authorizing the use of force in support of rebel forces. Other North Atlantic Treaty Organization (NATO) nations supplying warships and aircraft included the United States, Great Britain, Canada, Qatar, Norway, Italy, Spain, and Denmark. In early 2015, the *Charles de Gaulle* also joined the USS *Carl Vinson* in launching air strikes against the militant Islamic group ISIS (Islamic State of Iraq and Syria).

In sharp contrast to its primary military mission, the aircraft carrier often serves as an agent of humanitarian aid and relief. Carrier crewmen and air wing personnel have rescued countless sailors and civilians in distress on the high seas. Answering an emergency call from a cruise ship off the Baja peninsula of California in 2007, a helicopter from the USS *Ronald Reagan* airlifted a young man with acute appendicitis to the carrier, where the ship's surgeon performed an appendectomy. In October 2002, the *Charles de Gaulle* dispatched a helicopter that plucked three sailors from their small boat as it sank beneath them in the Mediterranean.

Since their earliest days, carriers have come to the rescue. In 1929, the electric turbines of the carrier *Lexington* supplied 30 percent of the electricity needed by the city of Tacoma, Washington, for a month after drought conditions caused water levels to drop so low that hydroelectric dams could not generate enough power. In 1954 and 1955, the escort carrier *Saipan* supported hurricane and flood relief efforts on the Caribbean island of Hispaniola and in Mexico, providing food, medical supplies, and fresh water.

During the height of the NASA space program in the 1960s and 1970s, US Navy *Essex*-class carriers were on station to recover astronauts returning from most of the missions of the Mercury, Gemini, and Apollo programs. In 1975, the carriers *Midway* and *Hancock* took aboard more than seven thousand American and Vietnamese civilians during the fall of Saigon to communist forces and the collapse of the South Vietnamese government.

The desalination equipment aboard a nuclear-powered aircraft carrier is capable of producing four hundred thousand gallons of freshwater from saltwater per day, while its food preparation area can serve up to twenty thousand meals per day. The medical personnel of a *Nimitz*-class carrier include more than fifty doctors, surgeons, dentists, and nurses. Its

A carrier variant of the F-35C Lightning II Joint Strike Fighter conducts its first carrier-based nighttime operations aboard the USS *Nimitz* somewhere in the Pacific Ocean in November 2014. Crewmembers observe the exercise from the Integrated Catapult Control Station (ICCS), a.k.a. the "bubble," unique to *Nimitz*-class carriers. *US Navy photo/Courtesy Lockheed Martin/Andy Wolfe*

hospital ward can be expanded to 150 beds with a three-bed intensive care unit if necessary in times of humanitarian crisis.

In 2004, the *Abraham Lincoln* responded to the devastating tsunami that struck Southeast Asia, conducting search and rescue operations and delivering supplies to stricken areas by air. When Haiti was hit by an earthquake that measured 7.0 on the Richter scale, the *Carl Vinson* spearheaded relief efforts with medical supplies, food, and thousands of gallons of drinking water. After a 9.0 magnitude earthquake and the following tsunami ravaged portions of Japan in 2011, the *Ronald Reagan* reached the coast of the island nation and rendered aid.

In November 2013, a massive typhoon wracked the Philippines. The *George Washington* led a relief force that included the cruisers *Antietam* and *Cowpens*, the destroyer *Mustin*, the supply ship *Charles Drew*, and the destroyer *Lassen*. Carrier Air Wing 5 flew relief missions to remote areas of the country for several weeks.

The versatility of the modern aircraft carrier and its ability to render vital services are readily apparent. In addition to providing security and offensive air power, and serving as a deterrent to aggression around the world, the carrier is involved daily with the business of saving lives.

A Grumman C2 Greyhound cargo aircraft takes off from the deck of the *Nimitz*-class aircraft carrier USS *Ronald Reagan*. The *Ronald Reagan* was among numerous US Navy assets that responded to stricken areas of Japan following a 9.0-magnitude earthquake and a tsunami that struck the nation in early 2011. *US Navy photo*

INTO THE FUTURE

Considering the continuing march of technology that inevitably may render some military platforms obsolete, the aircraft carrier has become the topic of serious discussion in recent years. With the development of sophisticated antiship missiles, the stealth of potentially carrier-killing submarines, and the advent of the unmanned drone aircraft that perform reconnaissance and attack functions, is the aircraft carrier at greater than acceptable risk in hostile waters?

Based upon an assessment of the continuing investment in the aircraft carrier by the United States, Great Britain, Russia, the People's Republic of China, and other nations, the answer appears to be that the perceived risk is acceptable in return for what the carrier may continue to offer those navies that deploy it. For the United States, the carrier remains the primary means of projecting military might over a great expanse of ocean in a rapid and efficient manner. The carrier may act as a deterrent to aggression just by its presence in a region where tension is high.

An aircraft carrier is, therefore, an instrument of political and military value. It provides the immediate muscle to back up the foreign policy of its government. It continues as the only viable means of placing offensive air power anywhere across the navigable oceans of the world. An aircraft carrier operating in international waters is the sovereign territory of the nation whose flag it flies. No permission to operate is needed. While friendly land bases may not be readily available, the aircraft carrier and its strike group are essentially self-sufficient for an extended period of time.

General John Shalikashvili, former chairman of the Joint Chiefs of Staff, expressed the value of the aircraft carrier succinctly. "I know how relieved I am each time when I turn to my operations officer and say, 'Hey, where's the nearest carrier?' and he can say to me, 'It's right there on the spot.' For United States interests, that means everything."

Since the great carrier battles of World War II in the Pacific, the tactical role of the aircraft carrier has evolved. During the last fifty years, the carrier primarily has functioned as a floating airfield capable of delivering air strikes against targets on land and sea within range of the aircraft aboard. Additionally, the carrier's aircraft provide security and protection for the other ships within the strike group and outside it. The planes also support continual antisubmarine operations. This tactical expansion has influenced design and cost, making the modern carrier the province of a relative few nations, most significantly the United States, which has the budget, the industrial base, the technology, and the global interests of a superpower at stake in the evaluation of the carrier's relative importance.

Still, the issue of high-tech weaponry that directly threatens the aircraft carrier remains to be continually gauged. At some point in the distant future, it may be that the aircraft carrier is so vulnerable to an array of weaponry that the waters in which it may safely operate, international or otherwise, are quite restricted.

Time and distance often dictate the best military option, and such conditions have certainly been apparent during the recently concluded Operation Enduring Freedom. Without a large number of land bases and considering the time necessary to deploy land-based squadrons in the Middle East and Persian Gulf areas, the aircraft carrier is the only platform capable of sustained flight operations on an extended basis. The carrier-based aircraft that took part in Enduring Freedom were often stretched to the limits of their range and required midair refueling, but they were effective.

Since the aircraft carrier's inception, ballistic missile submarines, more easily concealed beneath the sea, have supplanted the surface capital ship as the naval deliverer of nuclear weapons. In certain tactical situations, submarines and smaller surface ships are also capable of launching cruise missiles to strike targets from standoff distances without risking the lives of pilots or their expensive planes. Still, the aircraft carrier has yet to be deemed superfluous—and numerous nations are spending billions of dollars annually on new carriers and improvements to those already in service.

For nearly a century, the aircraft carrier has shaped modern history, and the useful life of the carrier concept may well last beyond the twenty-first century. For now, the aircraft carrier remains the most powerful warship afloat, and along with its accompanying strike group it will continue to serve as the frontline means of bringing air power to bear decisively around the world.

The USS *George Washington* is silhouetted as it transits the western Pacific Ocean at sunrise in July 2009. The *George Washington* was participating in an exercise designed to train Australian and US forces in planning and conducting combined operations. The march of technology has called the effectiveness of the aircraft carrier into question. For now, however, these warships continue to serve as the primary means of bringing air power to bear decisively around the world. *US Navy photo/Mass Communication Specialist 1st Class John M. Hageman*

This digitally manipulated image depicts a Harrier pilot's view as he prepares to take off from the deck of the HMS *Ark Royal. Defence Imagery/POA (Phot) Jonathan Hamlet/MOD*

INDEX

© 2016 Quarto Publishing Group USA Inc.
Text © 2016 Michael E. Haskew

First published in 2016 by Zenith Press, an imprint of Quarto Publishing Group USA Inc., 400 First Avenue North, Suite 400, Minneapolis, MN 55401 USA. Telephone: (612) 344-8100 Fax: (612) 344-8692

quartoknows.com
Visit our blogs at quartoknows.com

Zenith Press titles are also available at discounts in bulk quantity for industrial or sales-promotional use. For details contact the Special Sales Manager at Quarto Publishing Group USA Inc., 400 First Avenue North, Suite 400, Minneapolis, MN 55401 USA.

10 9 8 7 6 5 4 3 2 1

ISBN: 978-0-7603-4814-7

Library of Congress Cataloging-in-Publication Data

Haskew, Michael E.
  Aircraft carriers : the illustrated history of the world's most important warships / Michael E. Haskew.
    pages cm
  ISBN 978-0-7603-4814-7 (hardback)
  1. Aircraft carriers--History. 2. Aircraft carriers--Pictorial works. I. Title.
  V874.H38 2015
  359.9'48309--dc23
                                        2015030354

Acquiring Editor: Dennis Pernu
Project Manager: Madeleine Vasaly
Art Director: James Kegley
Cover Designer: Juicebox Design
Layout: Rebecca Pagel

Front cover: Commissioned in July 1992, the USS *George Washington* is the sixth of ten nuclear-powered *Nimitz*-class "supercarriers." When the massive Typhoon Haiyan devastated the Philippines in 2013, *George Washington* led the relief effort, delivering supplies and deploying search-and-rescue aircraft. The carrier is due for its midlife overhaul and refueling in 2016, a process that will take three years. *US Navy photo/Mass Communication Specialist Seaman Adam K. Thomas*

Frontis: A seaman watches a radar screen intently aboard the USS *Essex*. The lead ship of a legendary class of US Navy carriers, the *Essex* was laid down at Newport News Shipbuilding in Virginia on April 28, 1941, and launched in July 1942. Seventeen *Essex*-class carriers were built during World War II, and fifteen of them saw action. *The LIFE Picture Collection/Getty Images*

Title pages: The USS *George Washington* is underway near Guam at sunset. Commissioned in July 1992, the nuclear-powered carrier became the fourth US Navy ship named for the country's first president, a vocal proponent of a strong navy. *US Navy photo/Mass Communication Specialist 3rd Class Paul Kelly*

Table of Contents: With the Brooklyn Bridge and the skyscrapers of lower Manhattan in the background, the USS *Leyte* sails up the East River en route to the Brooklyn Navy Yard. An *Essex*-class carrier, *Leyte* was laid down in early 1944 as *Crown Point* but was renamed in 1945 to commemorate the Battle of Leyte Gulf. *Superstock/Getty Images*

Back cover: A boatswain's mate guides an aircraft onto a catapult aboard the USS *John C. Stennis* in the Gulf of Alaska in June 2009. The Stennis and Carrier Air Wing 9 were participating in an exercise focused on detecting and tracking units at sea, in the air, and on land. *US Navy photo/Mass Communication Specialist 2nd Class Kyle Steckler*

Printed in China